FROM COMBAT
to Client Service

A Guide to Hiring Military Veterans
to the Financial Services Industry

Jim Petersen, PhD

Standel Publishing

ISBN: 978-0-9969030-2-8

Table of Contents

Acknowledgments

My inspiration to write this book came from my many years of dedicated service in the military and the financial services industry. I cannot do justice in honoring all those who were an inspiration to me over this period of time. Countless people were constant sources of information and examples on how to recruit veterans of the United States military. Thanks to all of my colleagues, friends, and family for offering advice and keeping me motivated to pursue careers that I love.

The premise of this book was and is inspired by the dedication and service of the great men and women in the United States military. These professionals deserve to successfully integrate into civilian companies and industries throughout the world. In some small way, I want to give back to them for all they've given to me, my family, and our country.

I particularly want to thank Dick Cleary, who asked me to write *From Combat to Client Service*. Dick suggested making my master's thesis into a book at a time when I was looking for something to do in my next career. I deeply appreciate his inspiration and encouragement.

The initial inspiration for my first book, *Hiring Veterans*, came from Dr. Glenn Boseman when I was taking a course at The American College. Glenn handed me an article written by Michael Roney for a *Forbes* magazine special advertising section titled "The Business Case for Hiring Vets."[1] The title caught my attention, but I put it in a notebook to read later. I did not read the article until I decided to write this book and Russ Figueira of The American College gave me another copy of it.

During a discussion with Kevin Baldwin, it became clear that even though most employers want to increase their recruiting of well-qualified candidates, they do not understand the great opportunity that lies in the military market. Kevin has more than thirty years of experience in the financial services industry, and he has recruited and trained more than one hundred financial services professionals for a Penn Mutual General Agency. In addition, he has experience with Aetna, Lincoln Financial Group, and MassMutual. Kevin gave me the

---

1 . Michael Roney, "The Business Case for Hiring Vets," *Forbes* Magazine Special Advertising, undated, https://custom.forbes.com/2011/07/18/the-business-case-for-hiring-vets/.

v

Introduction

Most financial services companies do not seek out military veterans when recruiting advisors and other personnel to meet their recruiting objectives. Because of their intense training and high levels of responsibility that veterans are accustomed to, they tend to be reliable, efficient, and focused workers with a strong work ethic. They have been tested under very rigorous conditions, either during wartime duty or in support roles.

Recruiting veterans into our industry is an excellent way to pay back these heroes who have defended our country's freedom. We owe it to them to provide an avenue to further develop their skills in serving America while providing financially for themselves and their families. We have a unique opportunity to make service members aware of the variety of jobs and careers that are available in the financial services industry.

This book focuses on the tremendous opportunity that companies, firms, and agencies have to make veterans valuable members of their teams, and it provides guidance on the who, what, why, where, when, and how of recruiting veterans. This information encompasses many years of my observation and participation in military activities and recruiting military personnel. I am a veteran; I retired from the US Naval Reserve in 1998 as a captain (O-6).

To provide insight into the practical, real-life issues that military veterans face when transitioning into civilian careers—specifically in the insurance and financial services industry—I have included comments provided to me specifically for this book from a number of military veterans who entered this industry after separating or retiring from the military. I hope their experiences and the other information in this book inspire you to commit to recruiting and hiring military veterans.

Finally, regarding the military groups discussed in this book, most of us think of the military as active-duty personnel from the United States Army, Navy, Air Force, and Marine Corps. This book also includes the United States Coast Guard because this service increasingly provides support to our Armed Forces and has a mission of its own. This opportunity encompasses those in the Reserve and Guard who generally are civilians who support our military as necessary.

The support organizations have been a large part of our military. The sacrifices their personnel make are often equal to and sometimes greater than those of the active component of our military. In fact, the support provided by the Reserve and National Guard is so great that military personnel refer to the combination of active and reserve forces as a "combined force."

Now let's look at why veterans are excellent candidates for a career in the insurance and financial services industry.

CHAPTER 1

Military Veterans Are Ideal Candidates for Our Industry

The characteristics of a former, separating, or retiring military member are often what recruiters are looking for: significant leadership and life experiences, dedication to the organization and country, a proven track record in overcoming challenges, and the ability to make sound decisions in a fast-paced environment.

Ted Digges is the Executive Director of The American College Penn Mutual Center for Veterans Affairs, and he retired from the US Navy as a captain after twenty-seven years of service. He says veterans and active-duty military personnel are uniquely qualified for a second career in the financial services because they come from a can-do culture. "They bring so much to the table, and they're very comfortable operating in an environment that requires attention to detail and compliance," he says. "Plus, they are very comfortable working with different cultures and backgrounds. They are really well suited to be successful in our industry."

The military has already "separated the wheat from the chaff" and can attract recruits who encompass many of the characteristics mentioned above and who have matured beyond the level of their nonveteran peers. Often veterans are ready to take on a new challenge that rivals the dedication they provided to our country, having sacrificed their lives to protect and defend the United States and its allies in some very difficult situations. They are also motivated by making a statement personally, professionally, and financially as they transition into the civilian business world.

Military personnel eventually develop strong discipline that allows them to push themselves well beyond previous achievements; they realize that before they enlisted, they were using only a portion of their capabilities. Military personnel know what hard work is. Their days often begin around 5:00 a.m. and end at 10:00 p.m. or later. Military personnel are taught to solve problems quickly and effectively in life-or-death situations, build their physical strength so they can make it through difficult exercises and be prepared for combat, and work together as a team. This preparation makes them a wonderful talent pool for most companies and, in particular, to financial services companies.

One Manager's Profile of an Ideal Financial Advisor

Kevin Baldwin of B&L Financial Architects shared with me his ideal profile of a financial advisor. These characteristics apply to all candidates, whether or not they come from a military background, but most veterans exhibit these qualities:

- **Integrity:** Possessing and steadfastly adhering to high moral principles and professional standards
- **A focus on people:** A genuine enjoyment of being active within the community and working with individuals, families, and business owners to help them design, build, and maintain strong financial strategies
- **An entrepreneurial spirit:** Desiring to be in business *for* themselves but not *by* themselves
- **Self-discipline:** Being successful by consistently doing what unsuccessful people refuse to do
- **Relationship-building skills:** Having the desire and ability to build and retain strong relationships over time that are based on trust and integrity

Although Kevin's father and brother served in the military, he told me he did not initially consider veterans as a recruiting source. As we discussed this topic in depth, Kevin began to realize that he was missing a great opportunity. Most of us know and respect someone who served in the military. It might be a parent, a sibling, an aunt or uncle, a cousin, a business associate, a neighbor, or a friend. Often people we know credit their military service for making them more confident, stronger, and in better physical shape than they have ever been in their lives.

Kevin agrees that military personnel are excellent candidates for our industry because they have already been prescreened. The military will selectively remove people who are unable to meet the high standards required in the military recruiting and training process. Meeting those stringent military standards makes people ideal candidates for our industry because of the complexity of the advisor career.

I will make a note of caution here. The less time that someone is in the military, as in the case of some Reservists, and the longer the time a person is away from active service, as is the case for someone who separated years ago, the less value their military screening will have for managers in our industry. But those who have been in the military for a long time and those who separated or retired only recently likely have adherence to those high standards woven into their personas.

One of the qualities on Kevin's list is relationship-building skills. People in military units work extremely closely with their comrades and are responsible for their well-being, so relationship building is an integral part of the military culture. Military personnel are often thrust into tight living quarters and must learn to work together well. Also, because they are often far away from their families, they tend to build strong relationships with others that last a lifetime. That's something they might not have done if they stayed in the city or town where they resided for most of their lives.

The ability to build strong financial strategies needs to be explored during the recruiting process. Entrepreneurial spirit sometimes is ascertained by a military member's career path and jobs within the military but is generally not something that is part of military screening. For instance, Navy Seals and Special Operations personnel must often work independently or in small units. These top-notch forces are exposed to some of the harshest conditions. That makes them ideal candidates for running their own businesses, if they decide to do so. In

fact, many of them become independent contractors when they leave the service, often in the security protection business. I would put these Special Forces personnel in a distinct class and would definitely consider them as potential candidates for financial services.

The attributes of military veterans just mentioned are reason enough to commit resources to recruiting, hiring, and training veterans. Below are some additional compelling reasons to consider veterans for your team.

Military Training Tests Young People

A *plebe* is a freshman at a military or naval academy. "Plebe summer" is the summer training program that is required of all incoming freshmen at the United States Naval Academy. The program lasts approximately seven weeks and consists of rigorous physical and mental training. The purpose of Plebe Summer is to lay the foundation of the Academy's four-year professional development curriculum.[2]

A common question and argument among upper-classmen and graduates of US service academies is, "Did you have a plebe year?" This question might seem a bit odd to someone who has not witnessed or participated in the transition of a young civilian, usually right out of high school, into our military. This question encompasses many ideas and is the subject of much discussion and good-natured debate.

---

2. "Plebe Summer," US Naval Academy website, https://www.usna.edu/PlebeSummer/index.php.

4

Whether someone had a plebe year is really rooted in the question, "How difficult was it for you to transition into the military, and was it easier for you than it was for those who entered the military earlier than you?" It is always harder for people who went before you because entry standards have gradually been relaxed over the years. But no matter how much the standards have been relaxed, most people who are familiar with the grueling military training programs would agree that it is quite difficult to make this civilian-to-military transition. This question points to the key reason why there is such a great talent pool for financial services companies.

As I have personally observed and experienced, the plebe year, or the boot-camp experience, is designed to strip young people of their current identities for a period of time so that they can rebuild their identities and discover what they are truly capable of becoming. The newly indoctrinated person to the military must learn a number of skills in a short period of time. These young people are pushed beyond anything that most have experienced in their relatively short lives to find out what they can achieve—physically, mentally, morally, and personally. Many also develop their spiritual side because the tough rigors that confront them lead them to rely on a higher power to get them through.

Veterans Abide by Honorable Values

Evan Guzman is the founder of The MiLBRAND Project, which helps companies attract and retain veteran hires. He says the reason companies love to hire veterans is because of the values that military service instills in them. "Veterans are loyal, resilient, possess a strong work ethic, and are masters of teamwork," he says. "Companies know that veterans bring advanced experience in meeting mission objectives and will adapt those skills into their jobs." [3]

These characteristics of military members and veterans align with many of the characteristics that financial services companies are seeking. I recommend that you write down the most important characteristics you are looking for in a financial services candidate and then start looking for candidates to interview.

---

3. Abigail Hess, "The Ten Best Companies for Veterans," CNBC, November 10, 2017, https://www.cnbc.com/2017/11/10/the-10-best-companies-for-veterans.html.

Hiring Veterans Shows Our Gratitude for Their Selfless Service

In 2006, Anheuser Busch developed a commercial that instilled patriotic pride in many who watched it. In the one-minute commercial, a group of uniformed military personnel is walking through a busy airport terminal, apparently arriving stateside from duty overseas. As they pass through the terminal, a bystander stands up and begins to applaud the American heroes. Others gradually join in until everyone in that part of the terminal is standing and applauding. The only words appear at the very end: "Thank you."[4] It serves as a reminder that we all owe gratitude to our military heroes. The best gift we can give them in return is to provide them with fulfilling, rewarding careers.

There are many stories of people doing favors for military, such as people in the first-class cabin on an airline giving up their high-cost seats so that uniformed military can sit in the more comfortable seats. American Airlines has done much to ensure that our military gets recognized by giving uniformed personnel access to their private Admiral's Clubs when traveling to or returning from overseas duty. American Airlines also has some touching commercials that feature its "Putting Them First" campaign to honor our military service members.[5] This program allows uniformed soldiers, sailors, and airmen to board an aircraft first, along with first-class ticketholders.

Respecting our military personnel and veterans is the socially responsible thing to do. This is in stark contrast to the way our Vietnam veterans were treated on their return from the Vietnam War. Here is what Howard Sitikoff said in his writings on "The Postwar Impact of Vietnam":

> Another consensus also gradually emerged. At first, rather than giving returning veterans of the war welcoming parades, Americans seemed to shun, if not denigrate, the 2 million-plus Americans who went to Vietnam, the 1.6 million who served in combat, the 300,000 physically wounded, the many more who bore psychological scars, the 2,387 listed as "missing in action," and the more than 58,000 who died.

---

4. "Bud Commercial Army Tribute," YouTube, August 15, 2006, https://www.youtube. com/watch?v=Mq9yAauMEkA.
5. "American Airlines Commercial 'Putting Them First,'" YouTube, August 12, 2013.

Virtually nothing was done to aid veterans and their loved ones who needed assistance in adjusting. Then a torrent of fiction, films, and television programs depicted Vietnam vets as drug-crazed psychotic killers, as vicious executioners in Vietnam and equally vicious menaces at home. Not until after the 1982 dedication of the Vietnam Veterans Memorial in Washington, DC, did American culture acknowledge their sacrifice and suffering.[6]

Many of these veterans did not have a choice to serve in our military because of the mandatory draft that required young Americans to serve in the US Armed Forces. Selfish Americans ignored or insulted these American heroes as they returned. If our military personnel were recognized at all, it was not usually positive. In other words, we turned our back on them. I personally experienced this treatment of our military and believe that we are making amends as we honor our modern-day military and veterans by recognizing and thanking them for their service. This is healthy for our country and yet another reason why financial services companies should give strong consideration to hiring our veterans.

US Department of Labor: Ten Reasons to Hire Veterans and Wounded Warriors

The US Department of Labor has a program called "America's Heroes at Work—Veterans' Hiring Toolkit." The website offers a plethora of resources for civilian leaders to use in recruiting and hiring veterans and wounded warriors. The website lists the following reasons that this group of Americans can become stellar members of a civilian company's team:[7]

1. **Ability to learn new skills and concepts.** While in the military, service members undergo rigorous training programs to become experts in a wide-range of skills and concepts that can easily be transferred to a civilian work environment. The

---

6. Howard Sitikoff, "The Postwar Impact of the Vietnam War," English Department, The University of Illinois, http://www.english.illinois.edu/maps/vietnam/postwar.htm.
7. "Top Ten Reasons to Hire Veterans and Wounded Warriors," US Department of Labor website, https://www.dol.gov/vets/ahaw/topten.htm.

skills they have learned and applied in real-world situations in the military make them ideal candidates to enhance your organization's productivity.

2. **Strong leadership qualities.** The military trains service members to lead by example as well as through direction, delegation, motivation, and inspiration in some of the toughest situations imaginable. Service members are not only well schooled in the academic theory of leadership; they also understand and have used practical ways to manage behaviors for results.

3. **Flexibility to work strongly in teams or work independently.** Military training teaches service members to work as a team by instilling a sense of a responsibility to one's colleagues. In addition, the size and scope of military operations necessitates that they understand how groups of all sizes relate to each other and support the overarching objective. While military duties stress teamwork and group productivity, they also build individuals who are able to perform independently at a very high level.

4. **Diversity and strong interpersonal skills**. Service members have learned to work side by side with individuals regardless of race, gender, religion, ethnic, and cultural backgrounds; economic status; and geographic origins, as well as mental,

physical, and attitudinal capabilities. Many service members have also been deployed or stationed in numerous foreign countries that give them a greater appreciation for the diverse nature of our globalized economy.

5. **Ability to work efficiently and diligently in a fast-paced environment.** Service members have developed the capacity and time-management skills needed to accomplish tasks correctly and on time, in spite of limited resources and immense pressure.

6. **Respect for procedures and accountability.** Service members know how policies and procedures enable an organization to be successful, and they understand their place within an organizational framework. They understand the need to be responsible for the actions of subordinates, and they understand how to properly elevate issues through the proper supervisory channels.

7. **Hands-on experience with technology and globalization.** Today's military uses cutting-edge technology to maintain our dominance over the enemy in the battlefield. From communications technology to the security of computer networks and hardware, service members must stay aware of emerging technologies in the public and private sectors.

8. **Strong personal integrity.** Military training demands that individuals not only abide by a strong code of ethics but that they live it every day. Military personnel are often trusted with security clearances that give them access to highly sensitive information. An employee with a proven track record of trustworthiness is an asset to an organization.

9. **Strong sense of health, safety, and property standards.** Service members are aware of health and safety protocols, both for their own welfare and that of others. Individually, they represent a drug-free workforce that is cognizant of maintaining personal health and fitness. On a company level, their attentiveness and care translate into respect for employees, property, and materials.

10. **Triumph over adversity.** In addition to dealing positively with the typical issues of personal maturity, many service members have triumphed over great adversity. Service members have proven their mettle in mission-critical situations that demand endurance, stamina, and flexibility. Wounded warriors have overcome disabilities and/or acquired injuries (some that are invisible) through strength, determination, and personal conviction.

Do you know anyone who is serving or has served in the military? Chances are, that person is a hard-working, fiercely loyal, resilient, strong, and determined individual who adheres to admirable personal values. There are thousands of veterans who would excel in our industry. Let's seek them out and give them the opportunity to have rewarding, lucrative careers that enable them to continue helping people.

Acknowledging the great potential that military veterans have to add great value to our industry, why don't more companies hire them? We will explore some key reasons in Chapter 2.

CHAPTER 2

Why Some Companies Don't Hire Veterans— And a List of Those That Do

With so many capable, talented veterans transitioning out of the military, managers in any industry would be doing their teams and their organizations a favor by being more purposeful about recruiting veterans.

But American companies have a long way to go in this area. Barb Doyne, a US Navy veteran, points out, "In Israel, at the age of eighteen, the majority, with the exception of those who choose to be ultra-Orthodox Jews, are drafted into the service of the Israel Defense Forces (IDF). Understanding this, employers in Israel have created a pipeline to hire those transitioning, efficiently integrating them into their workforce, all while leveraging the skills they obtained while serving."

Barb notes that in the United States, less than 1 percent of the population serves in the military. She says, "Those transitioning service members make up only a tiny fraction of the workforce being recruited by employers. US employers often undervalue the skills our servicemen and women acquire while serving. The Department of Defense, working with employers, should help identify prospective post-military careers for those serving, as early as the time of enlistment/commissioning. There has been significant improvement in our veteran hiring over the past decade, but there is still room for improvement."

The following are some specific reasons why many managers hesitate to recruit and hire veterans. In my opinion, these "reasons" are all myths that need to be debunked.

Managers Think Veterans Enjoy Moving Around

Drew Vasquez, a financial advisor for First Command and a major in the US Air Force Reserve, says he has seen civilian managers hesitate to recruit veterans because they think they might leave the job soon after being hired. "Most military service members are used to changing bases and moving every couple of years," Vasquez explains. "Some civilian managers worry that if a veteran has moved around every couple of years for three decades, he or she will keep doing that and not stay in the civilian position very long."

But it's possible that a more stable work environment would be a refreshing change. Ask candidates during the interview process if they have moved around a lot and to what extent they enjoy doing so. More importantly, they often want to stay in one place to benefit their families so their children can have consistency during their learning years. Veterans may tell you they welcome the opportunity to stay in one place for a change.

Managers Think Veterans Will Be Lazy in Their Second Careers

Vasquez cites two more reasons why civilian managers are sometimes wary about hiring veterans. He says, "Some of my corporate-America friends who have hired military people say that some veterans may not be as motivated because they are receiving a guaranteed pension of $50,000 to $70,000. As a result, they get comfortable with that safety net, leading to complacency in their post-military careers. Also, someone who has been a senior-level leader in the military is used to having command and control, with people answering to them, so many

civilian managers worry that veterans might not be willing to start out in non-management positions."

Again, asking the right questions during your interviews can shed insight about candidates' desire to work hard and their coachability.

Managers Don't Understand Veterans' Résumés

Lida Citroën is a "reputation management and personal branding expert" who has years of experience helping military veterans transition to the civilian workforce. In an article for *Entrepreneur* magazine, she notes that the differences between military and civilian cultures create a communication barrier. She lists three reasons why veterans often have a difficult time making favorable impressions on employers:[8]

1. **They struggle to talk about themselves and their successes.**
   Veterans often say "we" instead of "I." Citroën says, "Hiring managers aren't looking to hire a squad or platoon; they want to hear about successes and accomplishments in the first person. If veterans can be empowered with the narrative and confidence to clearly and concisely articulate their skills, talents, and vision, they can position themselves to recruiters and hiring managers who will quickly see their value."

8. "Why Veterans and Civilian Employers Have So Much Trouble Communicating," *Entrepreneur* magazine, February 6, 2015, https://www.entrepreneur.com/article/242537.

2. **They speak in general terms instead of citing specific skills and goals.** Military service trains for adaptability and resourcefulness. Transitioning veterans tend to state their capabilities in general terms, such as "I can do anything. What do you need?" In comparison, civilians are trained to be concise, direct, and intentional in their career strategies. When veteran describe their goals and value in vague terms, it makes it hard for hiring managers to see where they can add value to the company.

3. **The military résumé looks much different from what a civilian hiring manager is used to.** Instead of a résumé, the military uses a Field Service Record to detail qualifications, training, and experience. Military terms, jargon, acronyms, certifications, and accomplishments often don't translate well from a military role to a civilian job.

Civilian recruiters can help during the interviewing process by prompting military veterans to describe their work experience, work history, and career goals in terms of their personal passion, vision, and talents. That way, the résumé is merely a tool that reflects who they are and where they can add value to the company.

I discuss this topic more in Chapter 4, "When and How to Recruit Veterans."

Managers Think Veterans Don't Have a Natural Market

It has been traditional in the insurance and financial services industry to expect new agents and advisors to come into their new careers with a "natural market." They are expected to launch their sales career by approaching the people they know and encourage them to purchase insurance and other financial services products.

Some managers in our industry worry that veterans who joined the military right out of high school or college won't have a natural market to get them started in the career. But the military offers an opportunity for agents and advisors to develop a military-related niche, which expands the number of clients available. Scott Kallenbach, FLMI, addressed this topic in an article he wrote for LIMRA titled "Niche Marketing":

Being a generalist requires a broad knowledge base that is difficult to maintain. It may be easier to focus on a few specific markets or products and develop an expertise, rather than try and keep up with all that is available. In an era of heightened compliance and suitability scrutiny, understanding the needs of a specific niche enhances the sales professional's ability to recommend appropriate solutions.

Becoming a recognized expert in a particular field can help sales professionals obtain referrals. Their reputation will precede them, and customers will respect their specialized knowledge.

Seventy percent of producers say they operate in a niche market. The decision to become a specialist is most often made in order to expand a practice or by seizing an opportunity presented by a new product or sales concept.[9]

Military personnel often have an extended natural market because many of the people they have served with live in various locations throughout the country. If the company, firm, or agency that service members are seeking to join happens to be near a military installation, then they have a natural market, even if they did not serve in that unit, grow up in the area, or represent that branch of service.

I believe military veterans generally relate better to potential military clients than nonveterans do. Potential clients with military backgrounds are often more willing to trust, and do business with, others who have served in the military. They share a common bond.

If you hire a veteran to serve a military installation, it is imperative that you follow the strict guidance regarding base solicitation. Each installation generally has solicitation regulations. A base solicitation officer can provide guidance about what is and is not allowed.

So what about veterans who do not live in the vicinity of a major military installation? Unless they have spent much time in the locations where you are hiring, it is easy to dismiss them as not having a natural

9. Scott Kallenbach, FLMI, "Niche Marketing," LL Global Inc., Strategic Issue Series, 2011.

market at first. But most veterans actually do have a natural extended market because of their participation in the military community. In addition to the traditional groups a new advisor might target in the civilian world, there are a number of niche markets that can make up a veteran's natural market. Here are a few examples:

1. Active military who are serving in the area, often as recruiters for the military

2. Veterans living in the area

3. People who served in the same or a similar unit

4. Veterans' groups at local colleges or universities

5. Reserve or National Guard centers

6. Military recruiting offices

7. The American Legion

8. Veterans of Foreign Wars

9. People who performed similar functions as the new advisor or agent did in the military, such as logistics, transportation, communications, administrative, training/teaching, and executive leadership

10. People who have relatives and/or friends who are serving in the military

Now, on a more positive note, let's look at companies in our industry that have established initiatives for hiring veterans and are setting the standard.

Companies in Our Industry That Are Getting It Right

Some companies in our industry excel in recruiting, hiring, training, and supporting military veterans and their families. The following are some of the standouts, listed in alphabetical order.

Edward Jones

More than 1,500 Edward Jones financial advisors have previous military experience. The company's training programs are designed specifically for people who do not have a financial services background but possess the skills and competencies needed for success as a financial advisor. It offers training programs that are tailored to fit the needs and experience level of each candidate in transition. During the process, Edward Jones managers will work with each applicant to identify the program that is most appropriate for him or her.[10]

The company has pledged a statement of support for Guard and Reserve employees. In 2014, CivilianJobs.com named Edward Jones a Most Valuable Employer for Military®, recognizing the firm's deep commitment to recruiting, training, and retaining military veterans as financial advisors.

Farmers Insurance

In the fall of 2016, Farmers Insurance launched a program that provides professional attire to military veterans to help them prepare for networking events, job interviews, and work. The program is called Suits for Soldiers, and the original goal was to collect 50,000 items to help veterans dress professionally. As of early 2017, Farmers Insurance agents and their staff members had collected more than 70,000 pieces of attire.[11]

---

10. "Opportunities for Military Professionals," Edward Jones website, http://careers.edwardjones.com/explore-opportunities/new-financial-advisors/support/military/index.html.
11. Recruit Military website, "Farmers Insurance Suits Up Transitioning Military," https://recruitmilitary.com/resource/737-farmers-insurance-suits-up-transitioning-military.

First Command Financial Services, Inc.

First Command's focus has always been on serving US military families.

First Command was founded by an Air Force Lieutenant Colonel named Carroll H. Payne in 1958. He worked closely with the families of several crew members who were killed in a training flight. He saw the survivors' financial difficulties and began thinking about how he could help military families avoid the same fate. In 1958, he began laying the groundwork for the company that would become First Command. It is obvious from the company's mission statement that it is committed to serving those associated with military service: "Coaching those who serve in their pursuit of financial security." The company's advisors specialize in serving service members and federal employees.[12]

First Command's senior leadership established a military advisory board that helps the company focus on military opportunities that continues to this day. The First Command website says military personnel are welcome not only as advisors but as potential clients. First Command not only knows how to find and matriculate military personnel; its leaders and advisors are experts when it comes to military matters.

The "Recruit Military" website lists all types of companies that have "made a major commitment to veteran hires." First Command is on the list, along with Allstate Insurance, Farmers Insurance, and PNC.[13] The "Military Friendly" website researches thousands of employers and schools each year so military veterans and their families can make informed choices about the future. First Command Financial Services, Inc., made the 2017 list of Military Friendly Employers at the Gold level, and USAA was ranked among the top ten employers on the list.[14]

Penn Mutual

In 2012, The American College Penn Mutual Center for Veterans Affairs was established through a $2.5 million gift from Penn Mutual. The center's mission is "to provide educational support and career opportunities to eligible men, women, and their spouses who have

---

12. "Our Mission," First Command website, https://www.firstcommand.com/about.htm.
13. Recruit Military website, https://recruitmilitary.com/companies.
14. "Military Friendly® Employers," Military Friendly®, http://militaryfriendly.com/employers.

honorably served in the Armed Forces." Its vision is "to empower deserving veterans with career opportunities, thereby infusing the financial services profession with a talent pool of determined, mission-minded individuals who will be vital to the economic integrity and sustainability of the profession."[15] The center provides educational scholarship opportunities for active-duty military service members, veterans, and their spouses.

Tom Harris, CLU°, ChFC°, FLMI, is the Executive Vice President and Chief Distribution Officer of Penn Mutual. He encourages leaders in the insurance and financial services industry to hire some of the 21.8 million military veterans who are "devoted, collaborative, hard-working, and enthusiastic individuals seeking employment in the United States." Harris says, "Throughout my career, I've come to learn that military veterans possess the characteristics of superstar associates in the making. They're intelligent, willing to put in the work, have an entrepreneurial spirit and a strong sense of purpose, and they understand the importance of collaboration and teamwork. All of these features are essential to a successful career in the financial services industry, which is why attracting and training former members of the military can really pay dividends."[16]

As mentioned earlier, Ted Digges became the Executive Director of The American College Penn Mutual Center for Veterans Affairs in 2013. He retired from the US Navy as a captain after twenty-seven years of service. He came to the Center through somewhat serendipitous events.

"I have always had an interest in investing, going way back to when I was in elementary school. I used to chart stocks on graph paper, so I always figured I would get into the financial services business," Digges says. "But one thing led to another, and I ended up getting recruited to play football at the US Naval Academy. After graduation, I received my commission with a five-year commitment as an officer. I really enjoyed serving, and I stayed on for a full twenty-seven-year career, retiring as a captain.

15. "About," The American College Penn Mutual Center for Veterans Affairs, https://veterans.theamericancollege.edu/about.

16. Tom Harris, "Let's Help Enlist Veterans in Financial Careers," Think Advisor website, March 28, 2018, https://www.thinkadvisor.com/2018/03/28/lets-help-enlist-veterans-in-financial-services-ca/?slreturn=20180327104222.

"In my last year on active duty, I was the president of a nonprofit organization in Hampton Roads, Virginia, with the Navy Supply Corps Foundation. It was basically for camaraderie, networking, and charitable endeavors. I attended a board of directors meeting in San Diego, and at that meeting, I met a gentleman who was on the board of The American College. He was talking about this new program they were starting for military who were interested in a second career in financial services. I cornered him at the break and said I was interested. That was exactly what I was interested in doing. He told me about the scholarship program, and I applied for it in my last year of active duty. I was accepted and started taking classes. In 2013, the College asked me to lead the scholarship program as Executive Director of The American College Penn Mutual Center for Veterans Affairs.

"Seven or eight years ago, people started recognizing that post-9/11 veterans were having a tough time transitioning into their second careers. The national unemployment rate was high, but it was 50 percent higher for post-9/11 veterans. Finally, it was recognized that, as a nation, we could do a lot better job of hiring veterans. I have found that financial services is a welcoming profession for veterans, but managers don't really know how to recruit them. We've come a long way in the past few years, but I still think that we have a long way to go.

"At The American College, we have full scholarships available for active-duty veterans and spouses, and there's no obligation. We are interested in not only honoring their service but also in giving them an opportunity to have a fulfilling second career. By getting education and completing designations through The American College, you can have a nice transition into a financial services career. Then you will become a real hot commodity to employers looking to hire because not only do you have that tremendous background that you gained through your military service, you have taken the steps to gain education within the profession, and maybe even gone as far as gotten a credential."

USAA

United Services Automobile Association, better known as USAA, has been serving the military since 1922. It was founded by a group of twenty-five army officers who wanted to insure each other's automobiles. The organization made it through the Great Depression and has grown to provide direct insurance and investment services to military personnel.

USAA has won numerous awards and is among America's most admired companies. The company maintains many military affiliations that assist in the search for military members. Here is a partial list of the organizations that USAA partners with:

1. Air Force Association (AFA)
2. Air Force Sergeant's Association (AFSA)
3. The American Legion
4. American Veterans (AMVETS)
5. Association of Graduates of the U.S. Air Force Academy (AOG)
6. Association of the United States Navy (AUSN)
7. Enlisted Association of the National Guard of the U.S. (EANGUS)
8. Fleet Reserve Association (FRA)
9. Ladies Auxiliary VFW (LAVFW)
10. Marine Corps Association (MCA)
11. Military Officers Association of America (MOAA)
12. National Guard Association of the United States (NGAUS)
13. Naval Aviation Museum Foundation (NAMF)
14. Naval Enlisted Reserve Association (NERA)
15. Texas Aggie Corps of Cadets Association (CCA)
16. Tuskegee Airmen, Inc. (TAI)
17. U.S. Naval Institute (USNI)
18. The United States Navy Memorial (USNM)
19. Veterans of Foreign Wars (VFW)

20. Vietnam Veterans of America (VVA)
21. West Point Association of Graduates (WPAOG)
22. Wounded Warrior Project (WWP)

USAA focuses on the backbone of the military with a website dedicated to military spouses. This site provides articles and materials to help those whose active-duty spouses are deployed. Military spouses also should also be considered when looking to fill open positions.

USAA is a great example of why focusing on military members can strengthen a company with highly motivated and successful personnel.

Western & Southern Financial Group

From 2012 to 2018, Western & Southern Financial Group earned the 2018 Military Friendly® Employer designation from Victory Media, publisher of G.I. Jobs®. This recognition honors a company's long-term commitment to hiring former military, having policies in place for Reserve/Guard members called to active duty, and offering special recruitment military programs. Also, Victory Media has awarded Western & Southern its Military Friendly® Spouse Employer designation from 2014 to 2018.[17]

A website called MilitaryTimes lists eighty-two companies that are considered "Best for Vets." Companies that made the list were ranked according to their practice of recruiting people connected to the military; company policies related to veterans, Reservists, and their families; and the organization's culture. The first company on the list is First Data, a banking and financial services company. USAA Insurance is in the number six spot, and a few banking institutions also made the list, farther down.[18]

With some strategic effort and a genuine commitment from the top levels of leadership, any company can become known as a leader in the effort to recruit, train, and retain military veterans.

---

17. Western & Southern Financial Group, "Military Hiring: We Value Your Service & Experience," https://www.westernsouthern.com/careers/field-careers/military-hiring.
18. MilitaryTimes website, "Best for Vets: Employers 2017," https://bestforvets. militarytimes.com/best-employers-for-veterans/2017/.

CHAPTER 3
Where to Find Military Veterans

As with any new market, you must learn the nuances and language of the market to be successful. A simple way to start out is to identify whether you have a specific group of military personnel in your territory, such as a military installation or a Reserve/National Guard unit.

If you don't know, do a Google search or contact a military recruiter in your local area. Make an appointment with the officer or senior enlisted in charge of the office. Tell that person who you are looking for and ask where he or she suggests that you find candidates. Often, military recruiters maintain relationships with people they or their office recruited, so they know who is going to separate and come back to the area soon.

Ted Digges, a retired US Navy captain who leads The American College Penn Mutual Center for Veterans Affairs, has this advice about where not to find veterans and a strategy for attracting veterans. "In my experience, job fairs aren't usually a good use of resources because you end up interfacing with a very small pool of candidates," he says. He recommends having a strong online presence so that military service members can find you easily. He says, "Many people find employers through internet searches today. Make sure you have a strong presence on social media and that your website has search engine optimization so that you'll be easy to find when people type in keyword searches to find you."

Consider Hiring Your Clients

Lindsay Blanton retired from First Command Financial Services in 2014 after spending three years as an Investment Advisor Representative and seventeen years as a District Advisor. He retired from the US Navy in 1992 after serving as a pilot and commanding officer. His wife, Dalise, also spent time in the US Navy and later became an Investment Advisor Representative and then District Advisor and finally a Certified Financial Planner (CFP) at First Command Advisory Services in Fort Worth, Texas, for more than twenty years. She retired from that position in 2017.

Lindsay's advice to managers is to consider hiring clients as advisors. "Get them involved in the client process, and not just for one year. They need to have been clients for two or three years or longer. Then they know what to expect. That's the most important thing. Get them to think about this career while they are still in the military. That way, they have time, while they still have an income, to get through a lot of the training and the licensing. Today, many people are unable to pass the Series 7. As a result, they have to wait a month before they can take it again. That stretches out the time frame. Also, each time you fail the exam, it's harder the next time. It's a daunting task for people who are newly exposed to the whole process."

Dalise Blanton said her time in the military, and later as a military spouse, made it easy to relate to prospective clients with military backgrounds. "Anything I recommended, I could, with great confidence, say, 'We personally own these financial products and know their value to the military family.'"

She also says advisors who were once clients themselves tend to have a deep loyalty to the company. "Young people coming out of college or coming from other careers don't have the allegiance to the company that advisors who are also clients do."

During annual reviews with clients who were going to be retiring or separating from the military soon, Lindsay and Dalise would ask if this is a career they might want to consider. They would send a letter to those clients who were two years away from military separation or retirement and invite them to a career night or to an informational meeting with the District Advisor. They also would ask their clients to refer to them their friends and associates who were nearing separation or retirement.

Build Relationships for Referral-Based Recruiting

When you start your search for candidates with a military background, you will meet people who want to help our veterans. Whether it is a military parent's group that is well connected in the community, a Guard or Reserve center, military and commercial recruiters, veterans, or centers of influence, it is likely that you will find sources who will help you with referral-based recruiting.

If you are near a military installation, the Transition Assistance Program (TAP) director will be an excellent source of referral-based recruiting. You can also submit job listings to the person in charge, who will post or distribute them. The TAP director will also periodically distribute résumés of people who are looking for careers. Check the US Department of Labor Veterans' Employment and Training Service (VETS) website to find people to consult (https://www.dol.gov/vets/).

If there is a college in your local area, check to see if it has a veterans' group. There is likely someone at the college or university who handles GI Bill matters. This person can put you in touch with veterans who are attending the college. Check for a Military and Veterans Resource Center.

Also, you can sign up with the Center for Veterans Affairs at The American College to become an employer who agrees to review scholarship awardees to fill positions within your company.

When teaching salespeople about prospecting, a common method is to ask them how many cars of a particular make and color they saw on the way in to work, such as a black Mustang. Most do not know because they were not looking for black Mustangs. Over the next few days, the salespeople are asked to look for that type of car, and then they notice a number of black Mustangs while driving.

The purpose of this exercise is to teach them that you have to look for something specific if you are going to be successful at prospecting. The same is true here for managers who are tasked with recruiting. There are multiple sources of veterans in your local area, but you have to be looking. Most areas have an employment commission that helps local people find jobs. This commission might have a special unit for veterans. You can also find these people through networking groups such as Rotary, Business Networking International, Chamber of Commerce, and social and fraternal organizations. The key is to start asking, and you will find multiple sources.

Other Recruiting Resources

The following are some recruiting resources that managers and veterans might find helpful.

For managers looking to hire veterans:

- **Military.com**—This is a primary resource regarding everything military. On the website at https://www.military.com/hiring-veterans is an Employer Resource Center where managers looking to hire veterans can post a job, reach the right veteran audience, and access resources to hire and support veteran employees.

- **The Value of a Veteran (VOAV)**—VOAV is a woman-, veteran- and minority-owned small business that provides human resources consulting and training for organizations that are seeking to improve support, recruitment, and retention of military veterans. The company was founded in 2007 at the height of the veteran unemployment crisis when it wrote and published the first guide for employers on how to recruit

and retain veterans and develop a veteran recruiting program. Since 2007, VOAV has had the honor of assisting more than 350 major corporations improve recruitment and retention of veterans. VOAV offers consulting, live webinars, on-site events and web-based training. You can download a free "Guide to Developing a Veteran Recruiting Program." http://thevalueofaveteran.com/about/

For veterans looking for civilian careers:

- **G.I. Jobs.com**—This website features a job board where veterans can find top companies looking to hire veterans. Since 2001, G.I. Jobs° has offered articles, tips, and online tools to help military transitioners explore different career and post-secondary education options. The site provides specific how-to advice on choosing a college, writing a résumé, and interviewing. The blog for military veterans is a great place to find transition-related content from those who have made the transition to the civilian workforce. https://www.gijobs.com/

- **Military.com**—This is a primary resource regarding everything military. On the website at https://www.military.com/veteran-jobs is a Veteran Jobs page where veterans can search for military-friendly jobs and get job-hunting advice.

- **MilitaryHire.com**—On this site are thousands of postings for jobs that are currently available worldwide. Veterans can post their résumés and search for jobs at no cost. https://www.militaryhire.com/jobs-for-veterans/

- **Military Officers Association of America (MOAA)**—MOAA is the nation's largest and most influential association of military officers. It advocates for a strong national defense before Congress, represents the interests of military officers and their families at every stage of their careers, and offers a wide range of personal and financial services exclusive to MOAA membership. http://www.moaa.org/

- **Military Transition Network (MTN)**—This disabled-veteran-owned company provides career coaching, recruitment, and job placement services. It delivers valuable consultation services, training, and education that is focused on career development and employment leads for veterans, service members, and spouses. https://www.militarytransitionnetwork.com/

- **Non Commissioned Officers Association (NCOA)**—The NCOA was established in 1960 to enhance and maintain the quality of life for noncommissioned and petty officers in all branches of the armed forces, active duty, National Guard, Reserve, veterans (separated and retired), widows, and their families. http://ncoausa.org/

- **RecruitMilitary.com**—This website offers its services free of charge to veterans and their spouses to support them during their job search. It hosts the nation's largest single-source veteran database, with more than 1,200,000 members. The organization publishes the nation's second-largest veteran hiring publication, *Search & Employ* magazine. Copies are distributed every two months, and a digital version is posted on the website, along with the VetTen digital newsletter. In addition, the group has produced more than 900 job fairs in more than 66 cities. https://recruitmilitary.com/

- **Service Academy Career Conference (SACC)**—Administered and supported by the Alumni Associations and Association of Graduates of the US Military Academy, the US Naval Academy, the US Air Force Academy, the US Coast Guard Academy and the US Merchant Marine Academy, this is the only job fair exclusively for service academy alumni. SACC allows candidates to interface with a large number of companies and universities, whose representatives are encouraged to have in-depth conversations with the candidates to evaluate their skill sets. Semiprivate interview tables are provided at each venue. By registering in advance, candidates have the opportunity to have their résumés reviewed by the companies prior to SACC. The companies are encouraged to reach out to the candidates and invite them to their booths. https://sacc-jobfair.com/

- **Transition Assistance Program (TAP)**—Veterans can find TAP on most military installations worldwide. Benefits Advisors serve as personal guides for veterans as they prepare for civilian life and to help them access the Veterans Administration benefits they have earned. Most VA Benefits Advisors are veterans or military spouses, so they can relate to the challenges veterans face. https://www.benefits.va.gov/tap/

For both managers and veterans:

- **The American College Penn Mutual Center for Veterans Affairs**—As mentioned, this Center is a resource for companies that are looking for veterans or military personnel. Candidates can sign up for a scholarship to get a professional designation and are tracked throughout their studies. When candidate finish their training, companies can review their résumés and consider them for possible employment. The Center's vision is "to empower deserving veterans with career opportunities, thereby infusing the financial services profession with a talent pool of determined, mission-minded individuals who will be vital to the economic integrity and sustainability of the profession." https://veterans.theamericancollege.edu/

- **Military Times Magazines**—The Military Times publications provide timely information for people serving in the major services. An edition for each service typically comes out weekly. These are great publications to find out information about a particular branch of service, find out about upcoming job fairs, and advertise your company. MilitaryTimes.com also publishes daily newsletters, video content, and podcasts, as well as a variety of special reports throughout the year, including the annual military benefits guide and the Best for Vets reports on education and employment opportunities. Many military personnel and veterans read these publications. https://www.militarytimes.com/

- **RecruitMilitary.com**—This organization's goal is to engage transitioning and civilian-experienced military veteran men and women in the most meaningful way. Veterans and employers are connected through the website, the magazine, or face-to-

face with employers at job fairs. This website now delivers services that were once offered on a separate site, CivilianJobs.com. This site was created to offer an online recruiting solution for candidates who are transitioning out of the military, as well as military veterans with varying amounts of business experience. https://recruitmilitary.com/

- **The Veteran Jobs Mission**—Formerly called the "100,000 Jobs Mission," this is the leading private-sector solution addressing US military veteran unemployment. It began in 2011 as a coalition of eleven leading companies committed to hiring 100,000 veterans by 2020. Since then, the coalition has evolved to more than 230 private-sector companies that represent virtually every industry in the US economy. The Veteran Jobs Mission coalition has collectively hired more than 400,000 veterans since it began. Now the organization has raised its goal to hiring one million US military veterans. Beyond their ongoing search for top military talent, Veteran Jobs Mission members are continuing to increase their focus on retention and career development of veterans in the private sector. This includes supporting veterans as they adapt to the workplace by establishing sponsorship and on-boarding training programs, as well as industry-based coalition subgroups to increase collaboration among members. https://www.veteranjobsmission.com/

- **HireVeterans.com**—This website allows a veteran to search jobs, find a job, and post a résumé. It also allows a recruiter to search résumés and post jobs. HireVeterans.com also conducts job fairs, both in person and online. This service is free to veterans, but companies must pay a fee. A review of the companies that are listed on the website indicates that banks are the primary financial services companies on the site. An advantage is that you can have an electronic feed from your website to theirs to offer jobs. https://hireveterans.com/

- **MilitaryHire.com**—This site also allows a veteran to search jobs, find a job, and post a résumé, and it conducts job fairs. The site also offers career coaching for veterans. https://www.militaryhire.com/

- **Social Networking**—Sites such as LinkedIn and Facebook are great ways to let others know that you are looking for veterans and to find out groups that are made up of military personnel or who target military personnel. You can search for groups such as Employer Partnership of the Armed Forces Group. If you are unfamiliar with these ways of networking, you can find out more by discussing this with someone who has an account or by signing up for your own account.

The following are specialty organizations that can help you recruit financial services personnel with military backgrounds:

- **Veterans on Wall Street (VOWS)**—This initiative is dedicated to honoring current military personnel and veterans by facilitating career and business opportunities in the financial services industry. Through a combination of educational initiatives, mentoring, outreach to the military, employee affinity groups, and an annual conference, VOWS promotes career development, support, and retention of veterans throughout the global financial services industry. http://veteransonwallstreet.com/

- **Vet Friends**—This site is designed to enable military veterans to reconnect with friends from their military days and to share memories. Veterans who are now in the insurance and financial services industry can use this site to find friends that they think would be good candidates for a job. https://www.vetfriends.com/

Personally, I don't think anyone will have any difficulty finding talented veterans to hire. If you focus on hiring veterans and seek them out, you will discover that they are everywhere.

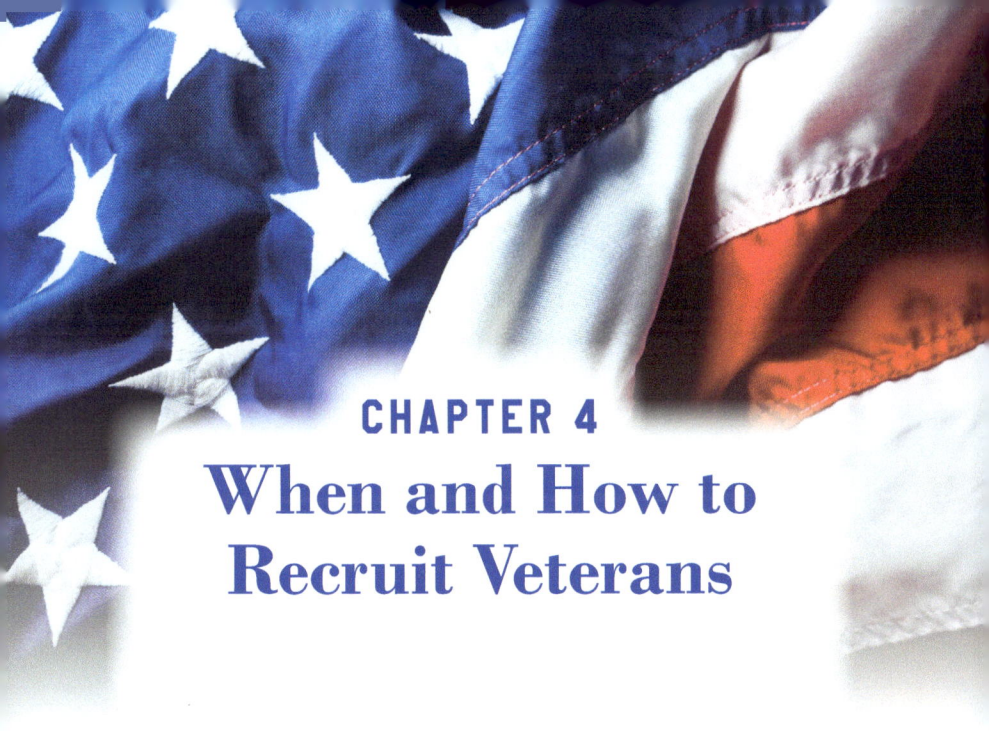

CHAPTER 4
When and How to Recruit Veterans

This process for attracting veterans is similar to the way you would introduce any new hire to the financial services environment. Effective techniques include having the new hire shadow established advisors or agents, setting up discussions between the new hires and longer-term producers, and checking in regularly to ensure that new hires are comfortable with the environment.

Job Factors That Appeal to Veterans

Military personnel come from all different types of backgrounds and have all different types of skills and interests, so we cannot generalize about what they are looking for in a career.

Many top-performing military personnel are interested in a career that challenges them like the military did. They tend to be risk takers who are ready to be their own boss, are disciplined to rely on themselves for success, and have the courage to face difficult and complicated challenges. My experience is that there are some who want the opportunity to move up in an organization at a pace faster than they could within the military and who look forward to getting rewarded financially based on their results.

I think that the veterans who have a desire to prove themselves are some of the best candidates.

Recruit Veterans Well Before They Separate or Retire from the Military

Because of the licensing that new agents and advisors must complete before providing financial advice to clients, the ideal time to find someone who separates or retires from the military is well before they separate or retire from their military careers. By getting the veteran licensed and trained in advance, he or she can focus on developing a natural market and building a clientele once on board.

Military members who are deployed in war zones likely have additional time to study industry-specific materials to get licensed or complete any training your organization provides, particularly if they can work on the training remotely. I strongly encourage you to minimize the down time as the service member transitions out of the military. It is very costly to hire military members, only to lose them to another company. Most military members who are best for this career will not want much transition time between the time they retire or separate from the military and the time they start on their new career.

An additional advantage when recruiting early is that many companies do not start making offers until about ninety days prior to the service member's separation or retirement from the military. Offering the military member a position as much as a year before he or she separates or retires gives your company an advantage. If the military member you want to hire is not fully engaged with your firm by ninety days before he or she leaves the service, you run the risk of losing that candidate to another company.

Ted Digges, a retired navy captain who leads The American College Penn Mutual Center for Veterans Affairs, says the sweet spot in terms of when to plan that second career is six months to a year from leaving the military. "There are about a quarter million people who are going through this process every year. They all have to go through a transition class. We market to those in transition," he says.

Dalise Blanton recommends starting to recruit veterans at least two years before they separate or retire from the military.

"It's going to take them at least eight months to get all the licenses they need. By starting before separation or retirement, they're not rushed," she says. "They cannot sit in front of a client until they're fully licensed until they are totally off active duty, meaning not on terminal leave. They have to have a complete separation. Starting them early in the process gives them time to sit in with a senior advisor or a trainer and work with the District Advisor to learn the process of interacting with clients. By the time they hang up that military hat and put on the civilian hat, they're ready to go."

Show Veterans How They Can Change People's Lives as Advisors

People who serve in the military are deeply committed to helping protect people, our country, and our freedom. They value security and responsibility, and they are highly focused on changing people's lives. Financial advisors change people's lives, too, but in a different way. Managers can attract veterans to the advisor career by showing veterans this strong parallel between the careers.

John Shull, ChFC®, is a leadership coach and speaker who completed a twenty-one-year career in the US Army as an Infantry Officer and Foreign Area Officer. For sixteen years, he served as a financial advisor and District Advisor at First Command Financial Planning.

John was a First Command client before he began his career there. "I was a new dad and an army captain. I had no idea what I was going to do to get this new child through college, so I was fortunate enough to meet what we called 'agents' at the time at Fort Hood, Texas, and became a client. Being a client was the important first step toward becoming an advisor. Being a financial services client before becoming an advisor is extraordinarily important. I had been a client for almost fifteen years when, in 1990, an agent I had been working with approached me about being an agent. I was about to retire with twenty-one years in the service. He offered me the opportunity to become an advisor, but I declined. My daughter was about to enter a private college in 1992, so I was taking on a huge expense. And I had two other children behind her. My thought was that I needed more money than what the career could offer.

"Fast-forward ten years. I retired from the Army in 1991. I went to work in a pretty secure defense contracting job, but not fantastically interesting, for four years. In 2000, I was approached one more time. By that time, I had been in two additional careers—with those four years as a defense contractor and about six more years as a management consultant with a small firm called Meridian Ventures. That firm was both successful and interesting and useful, but the partners began to stray from each other. I was traveling to California twenty-five times a year—150,000 miles of travel a year—way more than I wanted. So I decided to give the advisor career a shot.

"The first time I was approached to become an advisor, I could not picture myself as an insurance salesman. It's like Bill Murray's character, Ned, in the movie *Groundhog Day*—over and over again, he says, 'I need to sell you a bunch of life insurance.' That's how the general public can perceive agents, so I didn't think I was suited for that. I do understand the value of life insurance because I owned it at that time, and I bought more since then. There was a perception that it's a sleazy, slick sales position, but the reality is that it is a noble profession in which we change people's lives. In the military, we are changing lives by protecting people and keeping them alive. In financial services, we are changing people's lives by teaching them financial responsibility and emphasizing the importance of integrity and wise decision making.

"So in 2001, I connected those dots. I decided to become an advisor because I could see myself creating life-changing experiences for people. I think that is the best leverage as a theme for bringing on military people because the first thing veterans think about is providing security to people.

"I was with First Command for sixteen years and retired in 2016. I spent eleven of those years in leadership, as a District Advisor. I did a lot of recruiting during that time. Military people are focused on service. We're focused on taking care of people, taking care of soldiers, sailors, and airmen. We're focused on the mission, just like financial services firms are. I made it a point to explain to the veterans I interviewed to become advisors that this is not a sleazy sales job. It's a way of changing lives. It's a recasting of the military role of saving lives. In general, I think military people are very suited for this career because of their leadership experience, their go-getter kind of attitude, and their desire to avoid failing under any circumstances.

"There is a myth that military veterans are not suited for sales jobs. The way to get around that is to connect them to the leadership and service aspects of the sales job by first providing them with a good life insurance plan, a good investment plan, and a good savings and debt-management portfolio—as clients. Then you have changed their lives. Just like when you provide soldiers with the ability to manage their weapons and soldiers, you've provided them with ability to keep people alive. Those are connected."

Be Transparent About the Earning Potential

In general, military service members have their housing and health care provided for, so it might be a new and unfamiliar experience for them to realize that their mortgage or rent payments, health care premiums, and other living expenses will have to come out of their paychecks. It also will be difficult for many veterans to transition from guaranteed monthly income to irregular, commission-based income.

Many transitioning service members do not realize that it might take a few months to be hired by a prospective employer. When this happens, many are not prepared to cover their living expenses, which can be financially devastating. Barb Doyne, who separated after more than a decade of service from the US Navy, says, "Our veterans, upon transition, may face numerous difficulties, and without the financial resources immediately available, those issue may quickly become unmanageable. Not being able to care of themselves and loved ones has resulted in becoming part of this country's vulnerable population."

Because many veterans aren't sure how to transition into the corporate world, some take the path of least resistance, which in their minds is the Department of Defense (DoD) contractor jobs, according to Drew Vasquez, who is a financial advisor for First Command and a major in the US Air Force Reserve. "These positions are easy for them to transition to because they already know people at those organizations, or they already work with people who can help them get a job. So a lot of times, they take the path of least resistance, as opposed to an uncertain career path. Veterans who have already made up their mind that they will just coast in an easy job until retirement will not be convinced to anything else."

Vasquez says military veterans like the idea of a guaranteed income and the stability of staying with something that's familiar. "There's a huge fear of the unknown, which is big corporate America, sales, or starting a business," he says. "For decades, veterans have never known anything except good health benefits and a stable income. Being in their mid-forties or fifties and jumping into a second career where they might have to fight and claw to make progress and to make more money, or to work their way up, is something that veterans are either not interested in or afraid of. I think it's kind of a combination of both."

One day, Vasquez was telling the colonel he works with at his Reserve unit about this career and describing all the advantages. But the colonel said the same thing a lot of military people say: "I can't afford to not know what my income is going to be every month. I need a guaranteed income." Vasquez explains, "They're accustomed to bringing in maybe $120,000 a year. The idea of possibly making only $60,000 is crazy to them. They don't want to take on that level of uncertainty."

To help veterans overcome this fear, Vasquez recommends that managers who are recruiting military veterans point out to them that building up their income can take time. "They will understand that, especially if they were senior officers who were helping build up either a unit or a foreign force. Explain to them that it's not an overnight process. It's a long-term deal. It might take three to five years before they see real progress. Let them know that they could make double or triple the salary they started out with, which is a lot more than they could make taking a job in corporate America. In fact, advisors can easily make $300,000 to $500,000 a year while working only twenty or thirty hours a week. I don't think many managers are explaining the earning potential this way."

Leadership coach John Shull says managers need to "find middle ground" when discussing pay with candidates who are veterans. He says, "We often inform them about pay in two very misleading ways. One is to tell them that they are going to get rich quickly. When you do that, people are immediately disappointed that their income isn't immediately replicating what they were making before, on active duty. The second is to tell them that it will take a long time to build up their income, which often leads to them declining the job offer. Veterans want to make a difference in people's lives, so that attracts them to this career. But they still have to feed their families. The middle ground, and the most honest description, is that they will make a very good income as a financial advisor, and it will happen sooner if they work very hard in the beginning of their new career. This should be no shock to them, as veterans are accustomed to hard work and sacrifice, especially each time they hit a new military assignment and had to prove themselves all over again."

Also on the topic of pay, Barb Doyne, a US Navy veteran and veterans' advocate, says transitioning to the civilian workforce can be even more challenging for women because it is, for many, the first time they are going to be facing wage disparity. "The military pay system does not discriminate by gender; everyone is paid equally," she says. "Outside the military, here in the United States, most women are paid less for the same career of their male counterparts. One career that pays equally is that of the financial advisor. Advisors are paid based on performance, not gender."

Understand Each Veteran's Need for Benefits

If the veteran you are pursuing has already retired from the service, it is unlikely that he or she will need many additional benefits because a number of benefits such as health care are provided to vets. However, this might not always be true in the future because of budget cuts directed as part of DoD expense trimming. The military service member will let you know what he or she needs.

Some veterans have benefits through their spouse's employer. Because of the extended time away from the family and the extra financial pressures on all Americans, spouses often work to add to the family income.

Veterans have a pension that allows them to supplement any startup income they receive from a civilian company or from commissions. This generally enables them to be more financially solvent during the startup period and can help ensure that they stay in the career.

Also, some veterans receive a severance package that can include a large lump sum to assist with their transition. And almost all vets who leave the military will have government-sponsored relocation assistance, so your company won't have to pay that expense if the new hire needs to move to a new location.

Help Veterans Discover How Their Military Skills Translate to Civilian Positions

Ted Digges is the Executive Director of The American College Penn Mutual Center for Veterans Affairs. He retired from the US Navy as a captain after twenty-seven years of service. He says managers should recognize the great talent and skills veterans have but aren't aware of. "If you're a helicopter mechanic in the military, then you're probably going to be looking to be a helicopter mechanic in the civilian world," Digges says. "That's a 'hard' skill. But there are a lot of soft skills, such as communication and leadership, that can translate very nicely to financial services that are not intuitive to recruits or managers.

"Veterans have a wonderful background that brings in a lot of gravitas and world experiences that are very appealing to organizations and professions—but they can't always see the value of those attributes. Encourage them to think outside their comfort zone, to tap into their soft skills, and to reconsider going through the revolving door of a DoD career because those jobs are shrinking. Show veterans that they can start over fresh with a completely new career. If they have a pension, a built-in financial safety net, they can build a business very nicely."

For ten years, John Shull coached military veterans on determining how their military skills and accomplishments could translate to civilian jobs. "When people would ask me to look at their résumés because they were getting ready to leave the military, I would do so. Invariably, they always talked about their job titles rather than what they accomplished. A veteran would say, 'I was the Battalion XO.'

"I would tell him, 'Well, first of all, nobody knows what that is. Write down 'Executive Officer' instead, and then write one line about your duties. What did you achieve? Did you save the battalion training resources? Did you enhance morale or safety? Can you measure that?

Write measurable achievements that show some transparent connection to a business career.'

"They would go back to rewrite it, and it might take three or four tries. I coached one retiring officer who had been a ship captain. Clearly, it's a very big job to be a ship captain. I asked him how many people were on the ship, and he said there were 350. I said, 'That's great. What did you actually do?'

"He said, 'Well, I was the captain.'

"I said, 'OK, so what did you accomplish? What did you get your team to accomplish? How did you build morale? How did you build your teams? That's what businesses want to know about you. They don't care that your ship was 278 feet long and you were deployed for eighteen months and you were responsible for all these sailors. That doesn't matter. Managers in the civilian world want to know what your measurable accomplishments were and how you lead."

A tool called the Civilian-to-Military Occupation Translator can help you compare military and civilian job titles. It allows you to identify which military occupations (including Military Occupational Specialty, or MOS codes) best match your civilian job openings on the basis of education, training, skills, and experience. The tool translates civilian position requirements into the duties of many specialized

military occupations in each branch of the armed forces.[19]

Just enter the civilian job title or occupation you are seeking to match to military experience. Your results will list military job titles and military specialty codes that are a good match for your hiring needs. A search for the term "electrician," for example, returns a list of seventeen military occupation titles and seventeen unique military occupation codes, each closely related to a civilian electrician occupation.

Describe the Training Veterans Will Receive

Most service members recognize that although the skills they learned and used in the military were valuable in protecting their homeland, those skills might not translate well into civilian jobs. Be clear about the types of training they will receive, and assure them that just about everyone who enters the industry requires specific training in prospecting, sales, product knowledge, practice management, and client service—not just veterans.

Dalise Blanton says the managers at First Command went above and beyond to make her husband Lindsay's transition from the military easier. "There was constant mentoring, not only by District Advisors, but by Regional Advisors and other advisors in the office," she recalls. "They wanted us to succeed. Their objective was not to hire a bunch of people, throw them against the wall, and see who stuck. It wasn't a sink-or swim mentality. For that first year, Lindsay had someone sitting in on the client appointments he had scheduled. The Regional Agent would work with him and give him pointers. It was constant nurturing. That helps because in the military, you know exactly what your day is going to be like. So in his new career, it helped to have managers providing structure in his new position."

But Lindsay Blanton says that, unfortunately, that type of support is a thing of the past. "Things have changed. In many cases, profit has become more important than the person today. I think that breeds turnover in financial services companies that you didn't have before. And when you have a heavy turnover of financial advisors, then the clients are not as satisfied, of course."

This is sage advice for managers who want to take advantage of

---

19. Career One Stop Business Center, https://www.careeronestop.org/BusinessCenter/Toolkit/civilian-to-military-translator-help.aspx.

veterans' strong work ethic and talent. Recognize that veterans are accustomed to structure and knowing, at least to a certain extent, what their days and weeks will be like. They don't like to go into situations unprepared. Providing ample training in many different aspects of the career will put them at ease and give them more confidence from day one.

Veterans need training in this career just like other new hires do. Although veterans are taking a different path than nonveterans to end up in this career, they are starting out with little to no knowledge about it, just like all new hires.

Dr. W. Scott Davis, a sixteen-year veteran of the US Navy and an Associate Director of Field Force Training for First Command, says most of the skills people learn in the military are not translatable to civilian work, but veterans are accustomed to constant training. "There aren't a whole lot of civilian jobs where you kill people and break things, but military veterans are very teachable," he says. "There is constant training in the military. When they're not fighting a battle somewhere, which is 99 percent of the time, they're training for how to fight. So they understand training, and they adapt to training better than anybody out there."

Stress the Autonomy Advisors Can Have

A career as an agent or advisor will appeal to a veteran who wants the responsibility and autonomy associated with managing his or her own business. Be sure to stress the advantages of the entrepreneurial aspect of the business when recruiting vets.

US Air Force Reservist Drew Vasquez says that's what attracted him to his career in insurance and financial services. "I liked the fact that I could build my own business, make my own schedule, earn an unlimited income, and help people with something that I feel I am good at. I got my MBA while I was in the US Air Force. And I feel like I have a natural gift to help people make smart decisions financially. My wife and I got off on a good foot in our marriage, paying off some debt early on and then beginning to save. It allowed me to build up a buffer so that I could transition into the financial planning field."

Vasquez recommends focusing on this positive aspect of a career as a financial advisor during the recruiting process and say something like this: "Wouldn't it be fun to do something where you're making a real impact on families every day by helping them make smart financial decisions? And by the way, you get to spend more time with your family because you're not stuck at a desk from nine a.m. to five p.m. And your income potential is unlimited. If you want to work harder, you will make more money."

He also suggests presenting the career in a way that gives veterans a challenge to try something new. Although this career isn't as secure as what they've been used to, Vasquez says most veterans don't want to look back when they're eighty years old and say, "I never really took a step outside of my comfort zone to try something more dynamic that's a little riskier but could also have given me a higher reward."

Many veterans are looking to move up within an organization, so the career path might be important to them. Be open about what they must do to grow in the career and eventually transition into management. Just like any new hire, some veterans leave the career because they feel stifled in their ability to be promoted and compensated for the jobs they are doing.

In the military, expectations are extremely specific. So be specific when you explain to veterans how they can accomplish their career goals within your organization. Communicate why your opportunity is special in this regard. Many vets are extremely competitive and recognition-oriented. Tell them how they can compete and get recognized on a monthly, quarterly, and annual basis. Describe any contest and recognition programs you have in your firm or agency. Recognition in the military is not as individually directed as it typically is in a financial services company, agency, or firm.

Test Candidates' Aptitude for Meeting with Potential Clients

With all candidates, whether military veterans or not, one surefire way to gauge aptitude for the career is to send them out into the field to do fact-finders with potential clients. When candidates see what's involved, they will either be excited about the career or declare that it's not for them.

John Shull, a leadership coach and speaker, calls this process a "skill check," which is a term First Command uses.

John says that if he thought someone was a good candidate, he would conduct three interviews. In the first interview, he would ask,

"What do you know about First Command, and what would you like me to tell you about First Command?"

Then he would say, "Let me tell you how we connect with clients." He would take out a booklet and ask these four questions:

"If money were not an object, or an issue, how would you lead your life? What would you do?" It's another way of asking for goals without saying, "What are your goals?" People have a hard time with the goals question right away, until they feel they can trust you.

"What are your greatest financial fears?"

"How do you think you need to address those fears? How do you think they need to be dealt with?"

"How do you think a financial advisor, like me, could help you?"

John explains what he did next. "Then I would give each candidate seven of those booklets. I would ask them to go out and ask seven people those same four questions. It could be their spouse, another family member, even an adult child. Then I asked them to talk to their friends, coworkers, and keep going in concentric circles, farther out, until they reached people they didn't know very well and ask them those questions. I told them they could begin the conversation by saying, 'I'm interviewing for a job, and I've been asked to see if I could have a conversation about financial questions. Would you be willing to give me about fifteen minutes to do that?'

"I asked them to write down everyone's answers and then come back and tell me what the experience was like. The candidates would always ask, 'How much time do I have?'

"I would tell them, 'You have a year. You have a week. You have whatever amount of time you want. This is not my timeline. It's yours.'

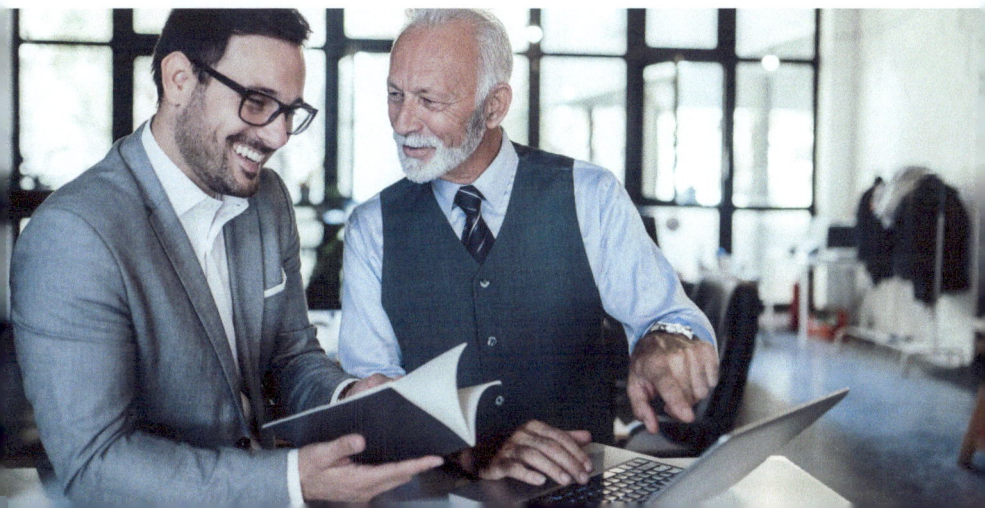

That was also a test. If they came back in a week, like many of my strongest candidates did, and were fired up and said they loved doing that, then that was a good indication that they would do well as an advisor.

"Some people would never bring the booklets back. I had a retired navy captain who came back with the seven booklets, all still blank. He was really sharp and was a long-time client of mine. But he said, 'I can't do this.'

"I asked why not, and he replied. 'Well, it's too invasive—just too personal.'

"I asked him, 'Well, what do you think financial planners do? This is our career. This is exactly what we're going to ask you to do every day—to conduct financial life interviews. Every time you meet for the first time with a client, you're going to have this conversation, whether or not you have a booklet like this.'

"He said, 'I just can't do it.'

"I told him, 'You know, you saved me a huge amount of time. I appreciate your coming in. It sounds like this is not the career for you. Thank you very much.'

"At that point, I knew that this retired navy captain probably wouldn't have been very collaborative with training processes in the office and so on, if he already decided he was going to be successful without even doing what we asked him to do."

The skill check allows candidates to find out what the job really entails, and it solidifies their commitment to the job.

Discuss the Type of Supervision the Veteran Can Expect

The type of supervision a military veteran will receive might also be of concern. Veterans have been exposed to a number of leadership styles in the military and might know exactly which type of management style works best for them—and which type doesn't. The relationship between the vet and his or her immediate supervisor is typically very important. Make this discussion a part of your interviewing process.

Ask candidates with a military background what style of supervision works best for them. Do they prefer minimal guidance and a hands-off supervisory style? Or do they prefer to have a close relationship with their supervisor as they learn how to excel in the new career?

Include the Candidate's Spouse in the Recruiting Process

In the military, every decision affects the family, so both spouses must be involved in every decision that affects income, time commitments, and geographical moves. So, when recruiting veterans, be sure to include their spouses, both during the recruiting process and after they are hired.

Most military families have to rely on both spouses to make decisions because they are usually living far away from family and friends, sometimes in other countries. Military couples share a dependence on one another that is different from other married personnel, who tend to stay in one area over their careers. The spouse can be a deal maker or breaker and probably has strong opinions about the job the husband or wife is considering. Emphasis on the family orientation of a financial services practice will likely be of keen interest to the spouse, as well as the veteran.

John Shull believes strongly in getting the spouse of a military veteran involved in the recruiting process.

"I have found that, generally, married advisors are more successful because they have their spouse's support," he says. "My wife helped me a great deal when I started out in this industry. I would get home, and she'd ask if I made a sale that day. When I would say no, she didn't say, 'You idiot! What did you do wrong?' Instead, she said, 'You'll make one tomorrow. Just keep it up.'"

Lindsay Blanton says his wife, Dalise, was an incredible support to him when he first made the transition from the military into financial services.

"Studying for the exams I had to take for securities and insurance licensing was a real task for me because I always found it hard to study, even when I was in college. It just wears me out," he says. "One of the reasons I got through it successfully was because my wife was encouraging me to stay on track. We had children in the house, so it was difficult. There were a couple of times when I wasn't sure if I wanted to go through with it. With her help, I was able to successfully transition. And I did very well over the first three-year period, partly because Dalise helped me in the office as a client-contact specialist. She recruited prospective clients for me and attended events. She really invigorated our business. And then she became a very successful advisor and a District Advisor, just like I was.

"It was a hard transition for me because the military was so structured. It was kind of like jumping into cold water. It was pretty daunting because we had three boys. I was trying to support the family, and we had one of our sons going off to college. The expenses were beginning to roll in. It was very concerning because retired pay then was about half what you got on active duty.

"After I passed the exams, those first six months were very stressful for me. Trying to build the business made me very concerned about success. That's where Dalise helped by encouraging me to relax and trust in the process."

Lindsay says that back then, you couldn't interview without your spouse, whether the female was coming on board or the male. "I think it's imperative that both be present during the interview process. Just like a military career, if the spouse doesn't like it, it's not going to work out," he says. "Either the new hire will quit, or their marriage will suffer. This is a tough business because it can take a while to build up your income."

Dalise agrees and adds, "If I'm working long hours and my husband is not encouraging me, I will eventually feel like leaving the business. The spouse must be involved in the recruiting process and the launch of the new career. Both spouses must be involved so they fully understand the mechanics of it."

A Six-Step Process for Hiring Veterans

The Department of Labor has a website called "America's Heroes at Work" that can assist you in hiring veterans. The website offers a Veterans' Hiring Toolkit that is composed of a six-step process to assist and educate employers who have made the proactive decision to include transitioning service members, veterans, and wounded warriors in their recruitment and hiring initiatives. This is a comprehensive way to develop a plan to hire veterans, taking into account many factors that might or might not apply to your recruiting situation.

I encourage you to explore this hiring toolkit online. Here are the six steps in the process, along with key components of each step.[20]

Step 1: Design a strategy for your veteran hiring program.

The steps in this section are a few of the basic elements to help you begin your planning:

- Become familiar with the benefits of hiring transitioning service members, veterans, and wounded warriors.
- Learn about tax incentives associated with the hiring of veterans and disabled veterans.
- Plan for results—start with the basics.

Step 2: Create a welcoming and educated workplace for veterans.

Creating a welcoming environment for veterans and returning service members doesn't take much effort, but it does take some thoughtful planning. Here are suggestions for how to assess your current processes and explore ways to include veteran-specific actions into your strategy:

- Develop an understanding of military culture and experience.
- Establish your company and its job application process as veteran-friendly.
- Learn the facts about hiring veterans with invisible wounds of war—work to demystify traumatic brain injury (TBI) and post-traumatic stress disorder (PTSD) in the workplace.

20. "America's Heroes at Work—Veterans' Hiring Toolkit," US Department of Labor, https://www.dol.gov/vets/ahaw/.

Step 3: Actively recruit veterans, wounded warriors, and military spouses.

Broaden your knowledge of how and where to find veterans—and consider instituting a few strategies to help veterans better find you:

- Determine employment opportunities, and create detailed job descriptions.
- Consider using military language in your outreach and job descriptions.
- Consider alternatives to full-time employment, such as work experiences, internships. and apprenticeships.
- Access credible resources to help you look for qualified veterans and wounded warriors who are seeking employment.
- Know what you can and should not ask during an interview.

Step 4: Hire qualified veterans, and learn how to accommodate wounded warriors.

Reflect on your onboarding strategies, and consider adding a few new elements to be inclusive of veterans, both with and without combat-related injuries:

- Create a culturally sensitive new hire orientation plan.
- Understand your responsibilities under the Americans with Disabilities Act (ADA).
- Consider disclosure concerns.
- Know where to obtain free, one-on-one guidance on job accommodations.

Step 5: Promote an inclusive workplace to retain your veteran employees.

As most employers know, retaining a skilled workforce requires effort after the hire. Retaining a veteran in the civilian workforce is not all that different from retaining other top talent. Most employees want to know and feel that they are appreciated, respected, and worthwhile to the team. Here are a few suggestions for being inclusive of veterans in your focused retention efforts:

- Place a value on military service.

- Expand traditional Employee Assistance Programs (EAPs).
- Develop and promote peer (vet-to-vet) mentorships in the workplace.
- Practice veteran appreciation, and promote a veteran-friendly workplace.
- Recognize that military families might have different needs than civilian families.
- Understand your responsibilities under the Uniformed Services Employment and Reemployment Rights Act of 1994 (USERRA). This is a federal law that establishes rights and responsibilities for uniformed service members and their civilian employers.

Step 6: Keep helpful tools and resources at your fingertips.

There are numerous resources available to help employers in their veteran hiring efforts, but not all employers know where to find them and whether they are reputable. In response, the US Department of Labor has compiled the following list of free, vetted tools and resources to keep at your fingertips. While certainly not all-inclusive, this list is designed to be a quick go-to reference guide of helpful sources of information related to veterans hiring, retention, and promotion. Go to https://www.dol.gov/vets/ahaw/Resources.htm to follow links to these resources:

- Keeping informed via social networking and e-news
- Resources on recruiting, hiring, and retaining veterans
- Answers to common employer questions about veteran and disability employment:
  o Workplace accommodations
  o Costs, liabilities, and return on investment
  o Candidate qualifications and capabilities
  o Stigmas about employees with psychological health injuries and mental health concerns
  o Staff training and disability-friendly workplaces

Now, let's switch gears a little for Chapter 5 and explore some strategies that can help veterans navigate the civilian world effectively.

CHAPTER 5

Advice to Veterans Seeking Careers in Financial Services

Military service members who plan to retire or separate from the military soon would be wise to start planning for that transition into the civilian workforce as soon as they can. It can be a stressful experience, and waiting until the last minute just adds to the uncertainty and stress.

And, even though asking for help can be difficult for self-sufficient veterans to do, it can make the transition into a civilian career in financial services much easier.

Ted Digges, a retired navy captain who leads The American College Penn Mutual Center for Veterans Affairs, reminds veterans that people will be honored to help you find your way in this unfamiliar environment.

"Whether you've served just a few years or completed a twenty-plus-year military career, it's a very exciting yet nerve-wracking time. It's like you're about to step on the liberty launch in a foreign port you've never been to. You're stepping out onto a moving boat that's jostling in the vast sea," Digges says. "I talk to transitioning individuals every week, whether they're active-duty service members, veterans, or their spouses who are looking at second careers. I always tell them, 'Don't be reluctant to ask for help. People want to help you. A couple of years down the road when someone asks for your help, you will want to help them, as well. Know that people will be thrilled to support you.'"

Network to Find a Career You Might Like

John Shull recommends that veterans who will be transitioning to the civilian workforce soon network with their colleagues to find out about job opportunities on the other side.

John says, "My last four years in the army, I spent at the Pentagon. In my nineteenth year of military service, I knew I would be getting out soon. So I got five or six of my good friends together every week for lunch. We would just have a brown-bag lunch in somebody's conference room and talk about jobs and résumés. The guys would say, 'Well, I'm talking to so and so. Who do you know there?'

"When I became a District Advisor, I advised my veteran clients to do the same thing. It's amazing how many took me up on it and discovered that was the best way to find a job—networking through the people they already knew to share ideas and best practices and to brainstorm and get jobs. That became a good way for me to find advisors, too. People realized that I wasn't looking for a certain type of person, but that I was open to anything and everything. So they would say, 'Well, there's a guy in my group who's thinking maybe he wants to go into financial services.'"

Describe Your Military Experience in Civilian Terms

Here are some suggestions to help ensure that civilian managers understand the value, skill, and talent you bring to the table:

1. Decide on a specific career path you would like to pursue, and then learn how to describe how your military experience has prepared you for that career.

2. Revise your résumé so that civilian recruiters can easily understand your accomplishments, skills, and goals. Get help with this, if necessary. Ease up on the jargon and acronyms. Get help from someone who understands both the military culture and the civilian culture.

3. Practice answering recruiters' questions in a way that positions you as qualified, capable, and able to transfer military skills to a civilian career. Role-play the interview with someone you know, if necessary.

Dr. W. Scott Davis completed a successful sixteen-year career in the US Navy. He now serves as the Associate Director of Field Training for First Command. Before he joined management, he spent seventeen and a half years as a field advisor. He has worked with and recruited hundreds of advisors who have made the transition from the military to the financial services industry.

He explains that, in all branches of the military, people who are getting ready to retire or separate from the military attend a weeklong class called TAP, which stands for Transition Assistance Program. It tells people how to transition out of the military.

"There is a book called *Navy Blue to Corporate Gray* that was written more than two decades ago, but it still holds. It explains how to transition from a military uniform to a business suit," he says. "One of the things they teach in TAP is, don't bring your military language into the civilian world. Nobody understands what you're saying. Another thing they teach is that the civilian world has a very different work ethic. You wouldn't think that that's a problem, but the military does not work 9:00 to 5:00. If you're in the military, you're working 24/7. They certainly give you a fair amount of time off. You can earn thirty days of leave a year so that you can completely go away. But even then, you're subject to being called back at any time."

Realize That Civilians Don't Share Your 24/7 Work Mind-Set

Dr. Davis explains that there is a big difference in the ways that military personnel and civilians view the work day. "Most military personnel get to work at 6:00 or 6:30 in the morning because that's when 'muster,' or roll call, is," he says. "They work until the job's done, so they might get done at 2:00 p.m., or they might get done at 9:00 that night and be back at 5:30 the next morning. They'll do what has to be done to get the job done. In the civilian world, it doesn't work that way.

"Civilians tend to watch the clock, and even during working hours, sometimes they're not working at full speed. They're taking breaks. And sometimes they're looking for ways to get around the job. Those who succeed are the ones who don't work that way, but it's important for veterans to know that most of the people they will be working with don't have that 24/7 work mind-set."

He advises, "If you want to stay in the office working until 8:00 at night, don't expect everybody else at work to do that, too. If you want to be the first one in the office every morning, you're not going to motivate everybody else to try to beat you in the office. It ain't gonna happen. In the military, the sergeant major will always try to find out what time the colonel is going to be there so he can arrive at least five minutes before. But that doesn't happen in the civilian world."

Be Willing to Do Some Menial Tasks

Dr. Davis says some military personnel, especially those who were high-ranking officers, find it difficult to succeed in the civilian workforce simply because they find it beneath them to do menial tasks that everyone on a team is expected to share.

He tells a story about one of his good friends who was the CO, the commanding officer, of the naval base at Newport, Rhode Island, named Captain Peter Corr. When Peter retired, he got a job with the city of Providence, Rhode Island, as a purchasing agent for the city. Every time Dr. Davis and his wife would go up to Newport to visit her family, he and Peter would get together for coffee because they had become friends on active duty.

Dr. Davis says that one day, Peter asked him if he remembered a particular two-star admiral. He did. One of the admiral's last jobs was as the commanding officer of the Naval War College. When the admiral retired, he asked Peter to help him find a job. So Peter got him a job with the state of Rhode Island.

The admiral lasted only two months in that job. Why? "Because he wouldn't make the coffee," Dr. Davis says. "Whoever would find the coffee pot empty in the break room was expected to make the next pot of coffee. But this guy was an admiral. Not only did he not make the coffee; he was used to having somebody take him a cup of coffee. It doesn't work that way in the civilian world. These might seem like small mind-sets that don't carry over from the military to the civilian world, but they can prevent someone from succeeding. This makes it tough for a lot of military folks, especially officers, to make that transition."

Continue to Work Hard

John Shull says he has hired some overconfident veterans who failed out of this industry. "They were higher-ranking veterans who weren't willing to do the work," he says. "You can make a quarter of a million dollars as an independent contractor in financial services, but only if you work your tail off and see clients, especially in the beginning. I saw clients every Saturday for two years as an advisor before I became a leader. And then I was in the office every Saturday for another year once I got into management.

"It was directly a result of hard work. Some military officers think, 'Well, I've done my hard work. I've put in my ten years and got out as a captain, or I put in my twenty years and retired from the military. I'm now ready to just make a lot of money.' That's very superficial and naïve."

John says the people he hired who were successful in this career were generally the ones who had a very good work ethic and understood that they were changing lives. "You have to have both," he says. "One of my best advisors was a young naval academy graduate in Annapolis. He is now in his seventh year. He is a wonderful advisor and is very well organized. Now, after seven years, he is making plenty of money, and he's working only the hours and days he wants. I would say he rarely works a forty-hour week. He spends a lot of evenings with his two young kids. Knowing that you're changing lives isn't enough if you're not willing to put in the work."

Refrain from Issuing Orders to Coworkers

Dr. W. Scott Davis adds that military officers also need to understand that they cannot issue orders in the civilian world. "You have to negotiate. You have to learn. If you're an officer, take a workshop in leadership because civilian leadership is a lot different than military leadership," he advises. "In the military, you can just issue an order, and as long as it's a legal order, the enlisted ranks have to go do it. But that won't fly in the civilian world."

Recognize That in the Civilian World, People Are Loyal to Themselves

Also, Dr. Davis says nobody's going to "take the hill" for you in the civilian world like they will in the military. "There aren't a whole lot of people who will follow their civilian leaders to hell and back, but they'll do that in the military," Dr. Davis says. "It's a different kind of loyalty. Loyalty in the civilian world is very rarely to the job or the boss. It's to individuals themselves, and that's a huge mind-set swing that military people don't have because in the military, everybody's dedicated to the country, the flag, and their branch of the service. In the civilian world, you are number one. You take care of number one. That's a mind-set that military people do not understand."

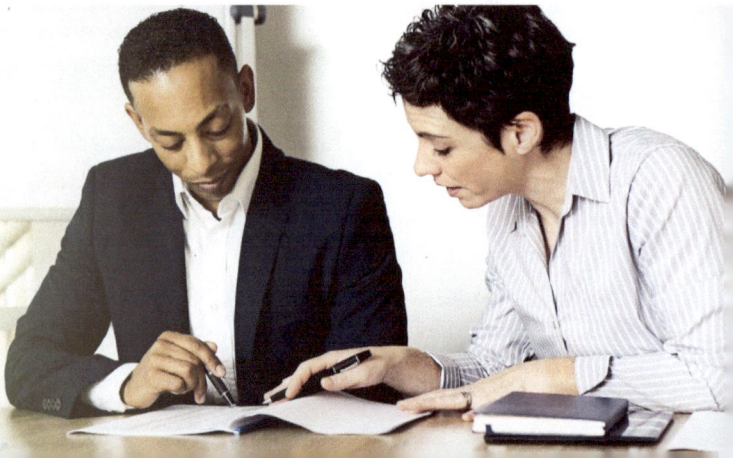

Be Aware That Evaluations Don't Always Follow a Protocol

"In the military, before a supervisor can write something negative on your annual review, there have to be at least two recorded incidences in which he or she has discussed the poor performance with you," Dr. Davis says. "If you respond and improve appropriately, then it goes away forever. If you do not, then it goes into an annual review, which is called a 'fitness report' in the navy. But in the civilian world, I have seen supervisors write negative comments in people's performance reviews without following that type of procedure. That will drive a lot of military guys up a wall, and you need to be prepared for it."

Recognize That Transparency Isn't Always the Norm in the Civilian World

Dr. Davis notes that in the military, because lives are on the line, 100 percent honesty is expected at all times. That isn't always the case in the civilian work environment.

He points to retirement seminars or dinners as an example. Advisors will advertise these events to retirees as sessions that will explain how to get their finances in order.

"But all they're doing is selling annuities. Every single one of them, 100 percent of them, they're only selling annuities. They don't have securities licenses at all. They don't have a Series 6, 7, or 66— any of the securities licenses," Dr. Davis explains. "They only have an insurance license because the annuity is an insurance product. It's sold by insurance companies, so they can sell annuities. But average investors don't know the difference. First, they don't realize that an annuity is an insurance product. Second, they don't even know what an annuity is or how different kinds of annuities work. They're hearing this agent or advisor who bought them a nice dinner say that this is the way to guarantee retirement income.

"It can be, but annuities are not appropriate for everyone. They're a great product when they're used appropriately, but these guys are all over the country. They're in every single town selling everybody annuities inappropriately. The securities industry is tightly regulated. FINRA is in your face constantly, but the insurance industry is regulated by states, by insurance commissioners. The only thing they are concerned with is whether or not an insurance company is charging enough money to stay in business because they don't want to pick up these policies on the state payroll.

"Some people get away with a lot in the insurance business. People coming into the financial services industry need to understand that just because their notions are noble, they might not be perceived that way. That's why I like working for First Command. We work primarily with the military, and most of us served in the military. We're going to take good care of each other, but not all companies and advisors are like that. One time, I heard a guy from a different company say at a conference, 'What we do is take *their* money and our experience and make it *our* money and their experience.' Unfortunately, that's what a lot of the financial services industry does. He thought that was funny. I thought it was pretty sad.

"You've got to be aware that if you're going to go into the financial services industry, that's the monster you're trying to tame. That's the lion in the cage that you're working with. The military is very simple and honest about what they do. There's no hidden agenda at all. We have a set of orders, and we execute them. Any questions? Go. But everybody has an agenda in the civilian world. Come into civilian life knowing that, and you'll be a whole lot better armed."

Plan Your Transition

Dr. Davis says that because nothing happens in the military without a plan, veterans are used to planning. And they need to formulate a plan for launching a civilian career after they leave the military.

He says it's important to realize that civilians often don't have a plan. "One of the biggest strengths veterans bring from the military is an ability to plan in great detail, down to who buys the paper clips," Dr. Davis says. "Your plan needs to include what your skill set is, what skills you need to gain, how many years you want to work, when you want to retire, and what lifestyle you want to have when you retire. Your civilian job hunt needs to be guided by that plan. Civilians tend to get a job first and then make their plan based on the job they happen to be in. I recommend doing the opposite."

Recognize Your Negotiating Power

Dr. Davis says military veterans are amazingly marketable, and they have more negotiating power than they think they do.

"Recognize the value of your skills, and use that to negotiate a higher starting salary," he advises. "My son, Adam, who works for Homeland Security, has learned already that if he's applying for a job that's advertised as paying $80,000, he can negotiate. He can point out that he has the right skill set for that job and tell the recruiter, 'I will do the job for you, but I want $90,000.' And many times, they will pay the higher starting salary because the candidate has the skills they want."

He adds that Adam has discovered the value of a good working environment coupled with a job you like. "Sometimes a little more money is not enough to draw you away from a really good position," Adam told his dad. "Military understand strong unit cohesiveness."

Dr. Davis says another point of negotiation is that military veterans already have medical and dental coverage, so they don't need it through their civilian employers. "You can suggest that your recruiter give you $10,000 a year more in salary because the company doesn't have to cover you on its medical plan."

When Dr. Davis was in the field as an advisor for seventeen and a half years, he says he saw so many clients coming out of the military, discouraged about their prospects of finding a job. He would tell them, "You don't have a clue how marketable you are, do you? Everybody's going to want you." He notes that in every single case where a client said that, they'd come back two months later saying they did get a job.

Transitioning from the military to the civilian workforce can be almost as intimidating and unfamiliar as being deployed to a foreign land. But there is no challenge too daunting for a US military service member or veteran! I hope these suggestions ease your transition into the civilian workforce.

CHAPTER 6
Employment Outlook for Our Industry and Veterans

An industry study conducted in 2016 revealed that, despite business growth, only 19 percent of advisory firms have a documented plan for future staff structure. The study also revealed that more than two-thirds of advisory firms think that it is becoming increasingly difficult to hire revenue-generating roles—lead advisors, associate advisors, and business developers. "Given the scarcity of talent available, firms are looking to new and nontraditional labor sources to fill the void," the report states.[21]

I don't believe there is a scarcity of talent at all. If companies, firms, and agencies would actively recruit military veterans, that would widen the candidate pool considerably. Firms need to approach organizational growth with specific and strategic objectives in mind. Why not set a goal for hiring a certain number of advisors or to have a certain percentage of your team members who are vets?

The outlook for jobs in the insurance and financial services industry is positive. At the end of 2016, the Bureau of Labor Statistics (BLS)

---

21. "FA Insight Study of Advisory Firms: People and Pay Executive Summary," TD Ameritrade Institutional, 2017, http://s1.q4cdn.com/959385532/files/doc_downloads/research/2017/FA-Insight_People-and-Pay_Executive-Summary.pdf.

reported how many jobs in specific industries were available in the United States, the median pay in 2016, and the job outlook for the next decade. Here is an overview of jobs in our industry:[22]

Position Title	Number of Jobs in 2016	Median Pay in 2016	Job Outlook, 2016–26
Personal financial advisors	271,900	$90,530 per year $43.53 per hour	15 percent (much faster than average)
Insurance sales agents	501,400	$49,990 per year $24.03 per hour	10 percent (faster than average)
Securities, commodities, and financial services sales agents	375,700	$67,310 per year $32.36 per hour	6 percent (as fast as average)

Also, the position of financial managers is expected to grow 18.7 percent from 2016 to 2026.[23]

As these numbers show, the opportunity is enormous.

The Jobless Rate for Veterans Has Declined

In March 2018, the BLS announced good news: the unemployment rate for veterans who served on active duty in the US Armed Forces at any time since September 2001—a group referred to as "Gulf War-era II veterans"—edged down to 4.5 percent in 2017. The jobless rate for all veterans declined from 4.3 percent to 3.7 percent in 2017.[24] In terms of comparison, the average annual unemployment rate in 2016 was 4.9 percent.[25]

---

22. Bureau of Labor Statistics, "Occupational Outlook Handbook," https://www.bls.gov/ooh/business-and-financial/personal-financial-advisors.htm.

23. Bureau of Labor Statistics, "Occupations with the Most Job Growth," https://www.bls.gov/emp/ep_table_104.htm.

24. Bureau of Labor Statistics, "Employment Situation of Veterans Summary," March 22, 2018, https://www.bls.gov/news.release/vet.nr0.htm.

25. "United States Unemployment December 2016," Focus Economics, https://www.focus-economics.com/countries/united-states/news/unemployment/jobs-creation-stays-solid-and-unemployment-rate-inches-up.

The number of active-duty U.S. military troops stationed overseas has decreased. The number dipped below 200,000 for the first time in at least sixty years. In 2016, there were around 1.3 million total active-duty US military personnel in the Army, Navy, Marine Corps, and Air Force. Of those, 193,442, or 15 percent, were deployed overseas. That's the smallest number and share of active-duty members overseas since at least 1957, the earliest year with comparable data, according to a Pew Research Center analysis of information from the Defense Manpower Data Center, a statistical arm of the Department of Defense.[26]

Recruiting Is a Challenge for the US Armed Forces

Recently, recruiting has been a challenge for the armed services. In 2018, the US Army is seeking 80,000 troops, which is 11,000 more than were sought in 2017. To reach a wider population of potential cadets, the army started accepting less-qualified troops, offering heftier bonuses, and granting more waivers for previously disqualifying things, like marijuana use and, in some cases, histories of mental illness. The Army was adamant that it was not lowering its standards; rather, it was changing the level of authority at which decisions about waivers for some standards were being made.[27]

Recruiting efforts have also been complicated by a robust US economy. Although the Pentagon has met its recruiting targets in recent years, low unemployment rates, common during the past few years, have been a hindrance. When the unemployment rate goes down, as it has been, military enlistment goes down as well, a military-manpower researcher at Rand Corp, noted.[28]

So why is it such a challenge to find new military recruits? The answer lies in the high numbers of young people who are obese, are uneducated, and/or have criminal records.

26. Kristen Bialik, "US Active-Duty Military Presence Overseas Is at Its Smallest in Decades," Pew Research, August 22, 2017, http://www.pewresearch.org/fact-tank/2017/08/22/u-s-active-duty-military-presence-overseas-is-at-its-smallest-in-decades/.
27. Christopher Woody, "The US Military Is Facing a 'Real War for Talent'—But Some Valuable Recruits Could Be Scared Away," Business Insider, March 14, 2018, http://www.businessinsider.com/us-military-war-for-talent-struggle-to-attract-immigrants-2018-3.
28. Ibid.

According to 2017 Pentagon data, 71 percent of young Americans between the ages of seventeen and twenty-four are ineligible to serve in the United States military because of inadequate education, criminality, and obesity.[29]

Most Veterans Leave the Military Before They Retire

The US military offered very generous pension benefits—after twenty years of service, members could retire with 50 percent of their final salary for the rest of their lives. That means most can retire around age forty, and the payouts are guaranteed for life. The military estimates that the net present value of its pension at retirement is around $200,000 for an enlisted soldier and $700,000 for an officer. This is enough for a basic living on its own, or more commonly used to supplement veterans' earnings in their second careers. But only 17 percent of active-duty service members stick around long enough to collect this money.[30]

Until recently, if military members left before twenty years of service, they didn't get any pension benefit. This leads to what's known as "cliff vesting" around the twenty-year mark. Because of the obvious dangers inherent in the service, and the stress it puts on families, attrition is steep in the early years. Then, near the ten-year mark, leaving rates flatten out. A large share of those who reach twenty years of service retire at the first opportunity and collect their pensions. The twenty-year point also often corresponds to a crucial up-or-out promotion point. Members who stick around longer can retire after forty years with a pension payout worth 100 percent of their final salary.

Major Brandon Archuleta, an expert on military retirement policy who teaches political

29. Thomas Spoehr and Bridget Handy, "The Looming National Security Crisis: Young Americans Unable to Serve in the Military," The Heritage Foundation, February 13, 2018, https://www.heritage.org/defense/report/the-looming-national-security-crisis-young-americans-unable-serve-the-military.

30. Allison Schrager, "Only One in Five People Take Up This Incredibly Generous Pension to Retire at 40," Quartz Media, March 14, 2017, https://qz.com/929153/only-one-in-five-people-take-up-this-incredibly-generous-pension-to-retire-at-40/.

science at West Point, says the pension serves as "golden handcuffs" for soldiers and officers once they reach the halfway-to-a-pension point of 10 years of service. "Once they get to that point, service members end up taking less-desirable assignments [instead of leaving the military], like Ft. Polk Louisiana, Korea, or Alaska."[31]

So what does this mean for recruiters in the civilian workforce? If only 17 percent of active-duty service members stay enlisted long enough to collect their pensions, that means that 83 percent of them are likely reentering the workforce. This gives our industry a huge pool of well-trained veterans to consider as agents and advisors. I encourage all my fellow industry leaders to commit to recruiting and hiring military veterans. Everyone will benefit!

The New Blended Retirement System (BRS)

To counteract the negatives of the previous all-or-nothing retirement system requiring twenty years of service for a pension, the National Defense Authorization Act for Fiscal Year 2016 changed the retirement plan for many service members starting on January 1, 2018. This new retirement system is known as the "blended retirement system," or BRS.[32]:

The US Department of Defense website that describes this system includes a BRS comparison calculator, a series of videos regarding the new system, a guide to BRS, and the policy that established the BRS. The policy states, "The BRS blends a twenty-year cliff-vested defined benefit annuity, similar to the existing uniform services legacy retirement systems, with a defined contribution plan that allows service members to contribute to a thrift savings plan (TSP) account with government automatic and matching contributions."[33] This action by the Department of Defense matches what many employers in the United States implemented over the past twenty years, moving away from a pension program toward emphasis on a defined contribution plan.

Although the purpose of this book is not to go into detail regarding these retirement systems, suffice it to say that the new system may cause

---

31. Ibid.
32. "Uniformed Services Blended Retirement System," US Department of Defense, https://militarypay.defense.gov/blendedretirement/.
33. Ibid.

some service members to stay longer on active duty to take advantage of benefits provided by the BRS. Because the system is new, it is difficult to say exactly what effect the BRS will have on retaining active-duty service members. I anticipate that this new system will have minimal effect over the long term, given the many other reasons why veterans leave active duty for civilian employment.

Even if the BRS contributes to service members staying in the military longer, civilian employers can benefit from the additional training and maturity of the departing service members. The service members who leave early and take full advantage of the BRS system by putting away retirement dollars will be in a better financial situation as they accept civilian employment. Those who stay for a full career of twenty years may or may not do as well under the previous system because of some of the uncertainties around the new BRS system. These uncertainties include the number of years served, the amount contributed to the defined contribution TSP, and the amount of the midcareer bonus, which will vary depending on the service member's circumstances at the time the bonus is activated.

To learn more about this retirement system, consult the Service Members Guide to BRS at https://militarypay.defense.gov/blendedretirement/. This guide does an excellent job of explaining the nuances of this retirement system.

CHAPTER 7

Understanding the Military Culture and Rank Structure

Before you start recruiting military veterans, do some homework so that you understand the rank structure and different jobs that military personnel perform. You can learn a lot about the military rank structure, pay, and benefits on the US Department of Defense website at http://www.defense.gov/. Here are some additional sites that contain a wealth of information:

- Officer Rank Insignia https://dod.defense.gov/About/Insignias/Officers/
- Enlisted Rank Insignia https://dod.defense.gov/About/Insignias/Enlisted/
- Military Pay and Benefits http://www.dfas.mil/militarymembers.html
- GI Bill http://www.gibill.va.gov/ (provisions of the bill in Appendix F)
  - o Post 9/11 GI Bill http://www.gibill.va.gov/benefits/post_911_gibill/index.html

 o Post 9/11 GI Bill Pamphlet http://www.gibill.va.gov/documents/pamphlets/ch33_pamphlet.pdf

The CareerOneStop website at https://www.careeronestop.org/, sponsored by the US Department of Labor, provides information on hiring veterans. Here are just a few of the many resources available on the website:

- Tools for exploring careers, including self-assessments, career profiles, and occupation comparisons

- Descriptions of various types of career training and information about scholarships and financial aid

- Job-search information about résumés, cover letters, job applications, interviewing, networking, background checks, and more

- An online search tool for finding US Job Centers by ZIP code

Recruiting someone from the military is similar to the process for recruiting anyone from a niche market. You must convince the recruit that there is an advantage to working with your company, compared to other companies. This might be simple if your company has strong name recognition but more difficult if it does not.

Interview Questions You Cannot Ask Veterans

Just as US laws prohibit employers from asking job interviewees certain questions about age or disabilities, employers also must avoid asking veterans specific questions. Here are some questions to avoid:[34]

34. Janet Farley, "What You Can't Ask a Veteran in an Interview (And What You Can)," ClearanceJobs website, August 30, 2013, https://news.clearancejobs.com/2013/08/30/cant-ask-veteran-interview-can/.

Do Not Ask These Questions	Details
What type of discharge did you receive from the military?	You cannot ask any questions about the type of discharge unless you work for the US government and are trying to determine a candidate's eligibility for federal employment based on various veterans' preferences. Federal contractors and subcontractors can ask about discharge status, but the questions must pertain to record-keeping related to veterans' preference or disabled-worker hiring requirements. If a no-federal job such as a contractor position requires a security clearance and the candidate doesn't already have one to begin with, you can ask about the type of discharge during the pre-employment phase.
Will you be deployed anytime soon?	Even if you see on the candidate's résumé that he or she is in the Reserve or the National Guard, you are not permitted to ask if he or she is going to be deployed. It is against the law to discriminate against someone who holds membership in the Reserve or the National Guard.

Do Not Ask These Questions	Details
<ul><li>Are you physically or mentally disabled?</li><li>Do you have PTSD?</li><li>Do you have any brain injuries?</li><li>Do you see a psychiatrist?</li><li>Did you get hurt in combat?</li></ul>	Asking veteran applicants questions about their disability is illegal, according to the Uniformed Services Employment and Reemployment Rights Act and the Americans with Disabilities Act. Here are some questions you can ask:<ul><li>Did you read the job description? How do your skills match the job requirements?</li><li>Can you tell me about your training and education?</li><li>What did you do in the military?</li><li>Can you do the minimum requirements for this job?</li><li>With or without reasonable accommodation, can you do the job?</li></ul>

About Specific Military Branches and Specialties

As I mentioned in the Acknowledgments, Kevin Baldwin, ChFC°, CLU°, Managing Director of B&L Financial Architects, was interested in recruiting veterans for the financial services industry. He asked me if some military branches or specialties are better than others for a career in the insurance and financial services industry.

My answer is that it varies. You can find excellent candidates among all branches of the service, so it is not necessary to limit your search to one particular branch unless your local market is predominantly occupied by a particular service. If you have a National Guard center in your area, hiring veterans who are familiar with the center gives them a natural market to start with. Even if your area is home to a particular service, most former military personnel are good at crossing the lines of the different services because many aspects of the various branches are similar.

Also, today many units are "purple" units, meaning that they are joint forces—a mixture of personnel from the various armed services. Many veterans who have served in one branch of service have served with military personnel in other services as well.

Military specialties can make a difference, depending on what position you are trying to fill. The US military provides a vast amount of training in a variety of disciplines. When you analyze the requirements of a job, you can then hone in on what specialty is best for your position. If you do not know, ask someone to help you understand the pros and cons of different military specialties.

Understanding the Military Hierarchy

It shouldn't matter whether you hire veterans who served as military officers or enlisted personnel, unless the position you are looking to fill requires prior leadership experience.

Given the diversity of occupations in the military, it is not generally a good idea to make a distinction based totally on rank when recruiting. Officers and warrant officers will typically have more leadership experience than enlisted personnel. But as enlisted personnel move up through the ranks, they take on more leadership responsibilities, and they might be just as qualified as officers for a leadership position particularly at the senior E-7 through E-9 ranks.

To better understand which categories of veterans to consider hiring, it helps to understand the military rank structure.

Military pay is based on military rank category. The three general military categories of rank (or "rate," if the military service is the Navy or Coast Guard) are Enlisted, Warrant Officer, and Commissioned Officer. Each rank comes with a distinct set of responsibilities that enable service members to fully contribute their talents to the military.[35]

Military Rank or Rate	Description
Enlisted service members and noncommissioned officers (NCOs)	Enlisted service members are known as the foundation of the military. Enlisted members perform the hands-on tasks of the military; often, these require specialized training. As you move up through the nine enlisted ranks, enlisted members assume higher roles for higher pay including supervision of subordinates. Army, Air Force, and Marine Corps Noncommissioned Officer (NCO) status—or Petty Officer as termed by Navy and Coast Guard—is the designation awarded to enlisted service members who have earned the highest ranks. NCOs have supervision duties along with their work as enlisted service members.

---

35. "Decoding the Military Rank/Military Pay Connection," Military Rates website, https://www.militaryrates.com/military-pay-charts-article.

Military Rank or Rate	Description
Warrant officers	Warrant officers are highly trained specialists. They can achieve higher roles within their primary specialties, providing management and leadership opportunities to enlisted members and commissioned officers within their specialties. To become a warrant officer, an enlisted service member must have several years of military experience, recommendations from his or her commander, and approval from a selection board. Warrant officers outrank all enlisted members, but they are not required to have a college degree.
Commissioned officers	Commissioned officers outrank warrant officers and enlisted service members, and they must have a minimum of a four-year bachelor's degree. Promotion through the ten commissioned officer grades is tied to the military service member's level of education, which is not the case with warrant officers. Commissioned officers can change positions within their specialty or be "non-line," which refers to an officer who is a non-combat specialist such as medical officers, lawyers, or chaplains. Commissioned officers are assigned through commissioning programs like a military academy, Reserve Officer Training Corps (ROTC), or the Air Force Officer Training School (OTS).

Understanding the Military Rank Structure

When recruiting military veterans, it also helps to understand the rank structure of the various branches of the US military. Here is an overview.

Warrant Officers

Warrant officers (CWO2 through CWO5) must have served thirteen enlisted service years prior to commissioning. They are specialists and experts in certain military technologies or capabilities.

US Air Force

The Air Force ranks share the same titles as the Army and Marines.

- **Company Grade Officers (O-1 through O-3):** The junior grades of officers in the Air Force often serve as more administrative leaders, though O-3s may be given authority over a company (becoming a "Company Commander").

- **Pay Grades:** Second Lieutenant (O-1), First Lieutenant (O-2), Captain (O-3)

- **Field Grade Officers (O-4 through O-6):** With continued areas of responsibility and sizes of commands, Field Grade Officers final rank of O-6 may command elements of a wing, while others serve as heads of staff in Air Force staff agencies.

- **Pay Grades:** Major (O-4), Lieutenant Colonel (O-5), Colonel (O-6)

- **Generals:** The O-8 is a two-star general and is the highest rank an Airman can achieve during peacetime. Ranks above this are picked by the president, temporary, and removed when they end their terms. The maximum number of four-star Generals allowed in the Air Force at a given time is nine.

- **Pay Grades:** Brigadier General (O-7), Major General (O-8), Lieutenant General (O-9), General (O-10)

US Army

The Army ranks are the same as the Air Force and Marines, except that, unlike the Air Force, the Army has a five-star "General of the Army."

- **Company Grade Officers (O-1 through O-3):** The junior grades of officers in the Army control progressively more troops, from generally 16 to 44 soldiers for an O-1, to company-sized units of 62 to 190 soldiers for an O-3.

- **Pay Grades:** Second Lieutenant (O-1), First Lieutenant (O-2), Captain (O-3)

- **Field Grade Officers (O-4 through O-6):** The numbers of soldiers led at these rank increase to brigade-sized units for O-6 (up to 5,000 soldiers).

- **Pay Grades:** Major (O-4), Lieutenant Colonel (O-5), Colonel (O-6)

- **Generals:** Generals in the Army start as Deputy Commander to the commanding generals for Army divisions. The Chief of Staff of the Army is a four-star General. A five-star general, or General of the Army, is only used in time of war.

- **Pay Grades:** Brigadier General (O-7), Major General (O-8), Lieutenant General (O-9), General (O-10).

US Coast Guard

Coast Guard officer pay grades are the same as the Navy.

- **Company Grade Officers (O-1 through O-4):** The approximate time it takes to go from O-1 to O-2 is 18 months. O-2s serve as billeted division officers, while O-3s are responsible for sailors and petty officers in different divisions. O-4s usually operate as mid-ranking officers in executive and command divisions

- **Pay Grades:** Ensign (O-1), Lieutenant, Junior Grade (O-2), Lieutenant (O-3), Lieutenant Commander (O-4)

- **Field Grade Officers (O-5 through O-6):** O-5s are the first Coast Guard rank to command ships or squadrons of aircraft. O-6s are given a high degree of autonomy in a variety of stations.

- **Pay Grades:** Commander (O-5), Captain (O-6)

- **Admirals (O-7 through O-9):** O-7s generally command small flotillas of ships, while O-8s command fleets of ships and air wings and are the highest Coast Guard rank during peacetime. The O-10 Admirals are the highest rank in the Coast Guard and report directly to the president.

- **Pay Grades:** Rear Admiral Lower Half (O-7), Rear Admiral Upper Half (O-8), Vice Admiral (O-9), and Admiral (O-10).

US Marine Corps

Marine Corps pay grades for officers have ranks similar to the Army and Air Force.

- **Company Grade Officers (O-1 through O-4):** O-2 is generally automatic after two years as an O-1. The O-3s act as Company Commanders for 62 to 190 Marines and are in charge of the tactical and everyday operations of their company.

- **Pay Grades:** Second Lieutenant (O-1), First Lieutenant (O-2), Captain (O-3)

- **Field Grade Officers (O-5 through O-6):** To achieve O-5 takes approximately 16 to 22 years of time-in-service. They command between 300 and 1,000 Marines. O-6s typically attend the Army War College.

- **Pay Grades:** Major (O-4), Lieutenant Colonel (O-5), Colonel (O-6)

- **Generals:** Generals in the Marine Corps start off by presiding over 10,000 to 15,000 Marines, and they are in charge of tactical planning and coordination of operations. Three-star generals (O-9) can only extend their status through an act of Congress. There may only be 60 total generals in the Marine Corps, and 3 of those can be four-star generals.

- **Pay Grades:** Brigadier General (O-7), Major General (O-8), Lieutenant General (O-9), General (O-10).

US Navy

The Navy rank structure is similar to the US Coast Guard.

- **Company Grade Officers (O-1 through O-4):** The O-1s and O-2s are often in schools for training or serve in the fleet as Division Officers. The rank of O-2 generally comes after two years' time-in-service (TIS). The O-3s are often Division Officers or service heads on some smaller ships, in aircraft squadrons, submarines, and ships. The O-4's serve as Department Heads or Executive Officers on a ship, aircraft squadron, or submarine.

- **Pay Grades:** Ensign (O-1), Lieutenant, Junior Grade (O-2), Lieutenant (O-3), Lieutenant Commander (O-4)

- **Field Grade Officers (O-5 through O-6):** As Senior Officers, O-5s may command a Frigate, Destroyer, Fast Attack Submarine, Smaller Amphibious Ship, Aviation Squadron, SEAL Team, or shore installation. O-6's serves as Commanding Officers of Major Commands such as Aircraft Carriers, Amphibious Assault Ships, Cruisers, Destroyer Squadrons, Carrier Air Wings, Ballistic Missile Submarines, Submarine Squadrons, SEAL Groups and major shore installations.

- **Pay Grades:** Commander (O-5), Captain (O-6)

- **Admirals (O-7 through O-9):** The Admiral ranks (also known as flag officers) are at the same level as Generals in the other services, and in the Navy command various ships and groups from an Amphibious Group, Carrier-Cruiser Group, to numbered fleets for O-9s. Assignments for Admirals (O-10) include Commanders of Regional Commands, Joint Commands, Chief of Naval Operations, and Chairman of the Joint Chiefs of Staff.

- **Pay Grades:** Rear Admiral Lower Half (O-7), Rear Admiral Upper Half (O-8), Vice Admiral (O-9), and Admiral (O-10).

Rank Factors to Consider when Hiring

Some enlisted personnel entered the service to qualify for educational benefits as well as to serve their country. Some just need a break from their schooling after high school or college to allow them to mature and develop additional skills before they address further educational needs or decide on a career. These are very sharp individuals who are willing to learn and will make great members of your team.

My experience is that both officers and enlisted personnel can be highly qualified for a sales position. You will need to do more screening of the junior enlisted personnel because many enter the military right out of high school, and if they leave the military in the first three to four years, they will be about the same age as many people who are graduating from college. Often, they do not have college degrees, and if the position requires that they have a degree, it is best to wait to recruit them until they finish their college education. For those positions that do not require college degrees, then there is no reason why you shouldn't consider junior enlisted personnel along with the other ranks.

If you are hiring for a position that requires a college degree, is more comprehensive in nature, and typically requires leadership experience, then I believe you should recruit commissioned officers, consider warrant officers next, and then look at senior enlisted who are consider noncommissioned officers (enlisted grades E-7 to E-9).

If you are looking for someone to start out by learning a specific product or service and who may or may not graduate to more sophisticated ways to work with clients, most ranks from enlisted grades E-5 through officer grades O-6 could fill such a position, if they have an interest in it. The more senior the position, the less likely that someone will fill an entry level position. The officer grades O-7 to O-10 are the flag officers who generally are not looking for entry-level jobs but are looking for senior management or board of director positions. Occasionally, a flag officer might become a producer, but generally he or she will use that job as a stepping stone to a more senior position.

At the other end of the military spectrum, E-1 to E-4, separating personnel are generally looking for entry-level positions that align with their military experience. These personnel might not be the best candidates for producer jobs unless they have some advanced schooling.

For those veterans who are interested in ending up in a specific geographical location that does not have or is not hiring for their military specialty, the separating person is often open to different kinds of jobs and might seek a job in the financial services industry.

Length of Service

A veteran's length of service can be either a positive or negative, depending on the position for which you're hiring.

If the job requires a mature person, it stands to reason that the longer the length of military service a candidate has, the more desirable he or she will be. If maturity is not a consideration, then the junior enlisted ranks (E-1 to E-4) are the only ranks that might require some special screening, in my opinion. The rest of the ranks should be considered. As I mentioned earlier, the lower enlisted ranks tend to be much younger personnel and should be screened as you would for anyone who is recently out of high school or college.

In the selection process, a better measurement than length of service is the veteran's personal motivation and desires. Some vets are not interested in a producer position but prefer a back-office support role. These veterans can still be of value to your organization; interview them for positions other than frontline production.

When to Consider Recruiting a Military Unit

In some cases, it might make sense to consider recruiting a "military unit" or integrate them with the other teams you are developing.

As a manager, I have had both a "military unit" district and one that was integrated. It is my opinion that recruiting military as a unit is generally a mistake unless there is a specific reason to do so, such as managing a business unit that targets a large military installation. If you are targeting a military installation, a specific unit of veterans allows them to concentrate on how they can market specifically to military and to use their understanding of the installation to find better ways to penetrate the market.

Another reason to hire a military unit is that if the group is of the same service and/or has experience in joint operations, its members might work better together when it comes to problem solving because they are accustomed to developing solutions as a team in the service.

Generally, most financial services organizations are not solely targeting a military installation, nor do they have the resources available to employ special units of military veterans. There is much that military personnel can bring to a financial services company, and there is much that military personnel can learn from others in the office. Sharing marketing ideas, understanding the various markets, and the overall strength of varying perspectives and ideas can result in a force multiplier. I highly encourage integration of military personnel because I believe it can be beneficial to all.

What if the Vet You Hire Is Called Back to Active Service?

This is a great question to ask because there is indeed a risk when hiring people associated with the military that they could return to active duty. Depending on the specialty of the service member, there is a chance that he or she can be called back to active service. It is less likely to happen to veterans who have retired from the military. It is rare, but conceivable, that a veteran can be called back to service if he or she has an unusual talent that is not available from others on active duty. Some military members who do not fully fulfill their active-duty commitments are allowed to separate as long as they stay in the Reserve or National Guard for a period of time.

But, as shown earlier in this chapter, the law prohibits you from asking veterans if they will be deployed any time soon.

Many Reservists and National Guard personnel stay in the active component of their respective organizations so that they can retire from the service and receive pay and most benefits when they turn sixty. These individuals drill about one weekend per month and go on active duty for approximately two weeks during the year to fulfill their obligations. Sometimes they volunteer to go back on active duty for as much as six months, which could be a disruption to their financial services practices.

Inactive Reservists and National Guard personnel do not participate in drills or go on active duty. These are the least likely personnel to be recalled to active duty because they require the most training to return to service. Also, they are often older than their contemporaries.

Although these issues can cause concern over hiring military, it is not as bad as it sounds. Given that the military will be looking at ways to significantly downsize over the coming years, it is unlikely that the government will let critical mission personnel go, only to recall them to active duty or to pull this talent from the Reserve and the Guard. Therefore, you are relatively safe in hiring military personnel.

There are unforeseen situations that could affect military members and veterans, such as the potential for future wars, conflicts, and tensions throughout the world that may require some temporary increases in active military personnel. But again, this is a very limited risk in the current economy.

CHAPTER 8
How to Make Vets Feel Welcome

When you have hired a military veteran, it is important to create an environment that is conducive to his or her success.

One strategy is to provide veterans with coaching and mentoring, just as you would any new hire. This type of specialized guidance can make the difference between success and failure.

It can be costly to finally hire a veteran candidate, only to ignore the important aspect of onboarding him or her. Let me stress that this is not just a challenge for military personnel but for anyone hired to fill a financial services position. The firms and agencies that have the highest retention rates of personnel in the financial services industry generally have strong onboarding programs.

Most military personnel are used to executing a plan or operations order. Many are good at fulfilling an itemized list of what they need to do. If you do not have a training plan for your advisors, create one. If you do, take a look at it to see if it addresses a situation that may take longer than the normal onboarding process that you experience. The reason for this is that some military members might be as much as a year from leaving the service due to deployments or the end of active service.

Integrate the military member or veteran into your group as early as possible. This will help him or her fit into your corporate culture. Not fitting the culture is one of the top reasons that veterans leave civilian jobs. Get them involved in your social activities, shadowing an advisor/agent, and even sitting in on appointments when appropriate. You will continue to receive input from people who observe the new hire in these settings. This input will also help screen the candidate to ensure that you have selected the right person for your team.

There are companies that can help you with the onboarding process. For instance, Military-Transition. Org (https://www.military-transition.org/) helps service members, veterans, spouses, and employers better understand and prepare for the military-to-civilian transition process and civilian employment. The Department of Defense often conducts Transition Assistance Program (TAP) briefings on many installations, which facilitate a smooth transition to the next career.

When you have the new hire in your office full time, the onboarding process is similar to the way you develop any successful advisor or agent. Feedback is important because most veterans do not have a sales-oriented background. Although they might have the attributes to be good at a sales job, many have not had to do it. Remind them that they actually *have* been involved in sales by selling their ideas, convincing others that their approaches to a problem are the right ones, or by convincing their seniors that they are the right person for the job.

Challenge: Do Your Part

Now that you have learned the who, what, why, when, and where of recruiting and hiring veterans, it's time to put together a business plan to take advantage of the opportunity presented in this book. Start with an assessment of your current situation. Figure out how military personnel can help your organization achieve its goals. Then determine how many veterans you need to reach your goals.

We often ask, "What's in it for me (us)?" Military personnel represent a significant pool of personnel who can help us meet our recruiting goals with quality, battle-tested personnel. In the spirit of Anheuser Busch and American Airlines, let's welcome home our military veterans and show them that we are willing to do our part to integrate them back to productive careers within society. To our military, we say, "Welcome home, and thanks for protecting us against enemies, both foreign and domestic, while showing us why freedom is not free!

We in the financial services industry can do our part to ensure that those who are willing to give their lives to defend our freedom do not come home to a lack of jobs or careers. These heroes can be the backbone of our industry for coming generations. Not only can veterans take care of our immediate recruiting needs; they can lead us to deal with the inevitable challenges of the future. In fact, the more companies that focus on our veterans, the easier it will be to convince these veterans to consider us for a career. It is the right thing for us to do. Let's each do our part.

APPENDIX:
Interviewee Bios

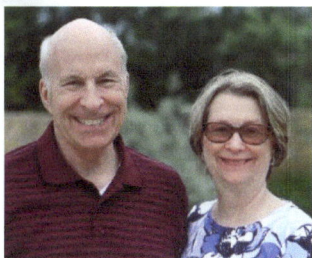

Lindsay Blanton and Dalise Blanton, CFP®

Investment Advisor Representatives (retired)
First Command Financial Services, Inc.

Lindsay Blanton joined First Command Financial Services, Inc., in 1992, after retiring from the US Navy. During his twenty-two-year career, Lindsay was a navy pilot and commanding officer.

During his twenty-year career with First Command, he was an Investment Advisor Representative for three years and a District Advisor for seventeen years. He was named District Advisor of the Year and was a GAMA International First in Class Award Recipient for First Command Financial Services. He retired from First Command in 2014.

Lindsay was born and raised in Charlottesville, Virginia. He played football in high school and college. He earned a bachelor's degree in political science from Hampden-Sydney College, a distinguished men's liberal arts college in Virginia.

Dalise Blanton, CFP®, joined First Command Financial Services in 1997 and was named New Agent of the Company in 1998. She was later promoted to District Advisor. She achieved her CFP® designation in 2014. She spent twenty years with First Command and retired in 2017.

Previously, she served in the US Navy and then became a career military spouse who was involved in military family activities, including T-ball, Cub Scouts, and tutoring students for whom English was a second language. Also, Dalise was employed with the Internal Revenue Service as an auditor and then as a Group Manager in the auditing division.

Dalise was born in Lincoln, Nebraska, and raised in Bluefield, West Virginia. She graduated from the University of Memphis with a BBA degree.

Lindsay and Dalise live in Fayetteville, North Carolina. They own a fine dining restaurant in Whitefish, Montana, where their middle son is the Executive Chef and a James Beard nominee. They have three sons and three grandchildren.

Winfield Scott Davis, PhD

Financial Planning Consultant
First Command Financial Services, Inc.
Fort Worth, Texas

Dr. W. Scott Davis served our country in the US Navy for sixteen years and was in the Chaplain Corps. He retired under the Temporary Early Retirement Authority (TERA) during the drawdown in the 1990s. He joined First Command in 1998 as an advisor and was soon promoted into management. Since 2015, he has served as the Associate Director, Training Delivery, and as the Associate Director, Field Force Training, for First Command Financial Services, Inc.

A graduate of Trinity College of the Bible and Trinity Theological Seminary, he also serves as Associate Pastor of Foundry United Methodist Church in Fort Worth, Texas. He was ordained as a minister in the United Methodist Church in 1977.

Dr. Davis holds a PhD in philosophy from Trinity College of the Bible and Trinity Theological Seminary, a master's degree in public administration from Troy State University, and a master's degree in telecommunications from Texas Tech University, a master's degree in divinity from Vanderbilt University, and a bachelor's degree from Scarritt College in Nashville, Tennessee.

Before joining the military, Dr. Davis enjoyed notoriety as Mickey Metro, the name he used while serving as a well-known DJ for a rock-music radio station in Nashville.

He and his wife, Myra, have two sons. Christopher is a Captain in the US Marine Corps, and Adam works for Homeland Security in Washington, DC.

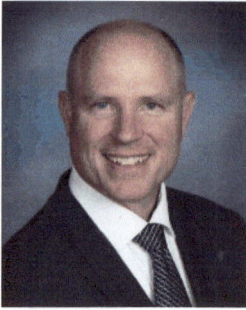

Ted Digges, Captain, SC, USN (Ret.)

**Executive Director, The American College
Penn Mutual Center for Veterans Affairs
Bryn Mawr, Pennsylvania**

As Executive Director at The American College of Financial Services, Ted Digges leads an organization focused on empowering active duty, veterans, and their spouses interested in a second career in the financial services profession by providing full-scholarship educational support and career opportunities.

He also serves as an adjunct professor at The American College, teaching a course on Decision-Making Leadership Skills in the Master of Science in Management (MSM) curriculum.

Formerly, Ted developed effective strategies for high-net-worth clients as a financial advisor with Merrill Lynch Wealth Management. Prior to that, Ted was president of a nonprofit organization in Hampton Roads, Virginia, focused on engaging the military community and charitable endeavors.

His broad knowledge in strategic planning, customer service, and program management was honed over a twenty-seven-year active-duty career. A retired US Navy captain, he served both in surface ships and submarines and was designated a Joint Qualified Officer, serving all over the United States, as well as in the Asia Pacific and Europe.

Ted is a graduate of the US Naval Academy and holds a Master of Science in Management and a master's degree in national security and international studies. He is a graduate of the Darden School's Executive Program at the University of Virginia. He holds the Certified Professional Logistician (CPL) and the Chartered Financial Consultant (ChFC) designations.

Barb Doyne

Registered Representative
First Command Financial Services
Orlando, Florida

Since 2016, Barb Doyne has served as a Regional Economic and Employment Liaison for the Veterans Economic Communities Initiative (VECI) at the US Department of Veterans Affairs in Washington, DC. As the VECI program lead in Philadelphia market, she works with multiple stakeholders to improve the economic landscape and outcomes for veterans and their families in local communities.

In 2013, Barb founded 5-Star Women, a national nonprofit dedicated to enabling women veterans to thrive in key areas in post-military life (family, health, career, education, and housing). Within its first month, US Senator Pat Toomey (R–PA) recognized the organization for its support of this important population. In 2015, the *Philadelphia Business Journal* named Barb as a Veteran of Influence.

Barb served in the US Navy from 1981 to 1994. She advanced through the enlisted ranks to become a Commissioned Officer and had assignments in Washington, DC; Monterey, California; Newport, Rhode Island; Atsugi, Japan; and Sinop, Turkey. She was awarded two Navy Commendation Medals as the first female Special Airborne Communications Evaluator and for developing a canvas response to a congressionally mandated, Armed Forces-wide cryptologic training review. She oversaw the training, development, and operations of more than eighty personnel in five different military occupational specialties such as linguists, Morse Code specialists, and electronic intelligence specialists.

Barb holds a BBA degree in business from National University in San Diego, California, and an MBA from the Washington, DC, campus of the Florida Institute of Technology in Melbourne.

John Shull, ChFC®
Leadership Coach and Speaker

John Shull has completed three careers in leadership positions and activities, beginning with a twenty-one-year career in the US Army, where he commanded soldiers and led military organizations as an Infantry Officer and Foreign Area Officer. His service included assignments in Germany, Korea, the former Soviet Union, Eastern Europe, and the United States.

Next, he held a leadership position in a small management consulting firm, Meridian Ventures, Inc., where he led engagement teams in solving key client issues in international energy, manufacturing, defense aerospace, and retail. For the next sixteen years, John served as a financial advisor and frontline manager at First Command Financial Planning. He was able to leverage his US Army leadership experience and knowledge to serve the primary client base for First Command—military service members and their families.

As a District Advisor at First Command, John managed three offices in two states. He grew his advisor force from four advisors to eleven and added an office. He created a model for district quarterly training, bringing together four districts to create greater collaboration among advisors on best practices and to build team synergies between managers. He developed a prototype for an advisor team leader to assist frontline managers with critical functional activities such as marketing, recruiting, and training and to recruit and cultivate new leaders for the company. Two of his advisors were promoted through that process. In 2011, John was selected from among sixty-five advisors as the First Command District Advisor of the Year and won the company's GAMA International First in Class Award in 2012.

John is currently a member of the Alumni Board of the American College of Financial Services and is an engagement speaker for the First Command Educational Foundation.

Drew Vasquez

Financial Advisor
First Command Financial Services, Inc.
Tampa, Florida

Drew Vasquez joined First Command Financial Services, Inc., as a financial advisor in 2013, following six years of service in the US Air Force. Currently, he is a major in the US Air Force Reserve.

His service included three years managing budgets exceeding $10 million for the 6th Air Mobility Wing, followed by six months in Afghanistan as the comptroller for a special operations task force, for which he earned the Bronze Star Medal. Finally, he spent two years as the chief of Unconventional Warfare Budgets for the US Special Operations Command, where he advocated to Congress for—and managed—budgets totaling more than $100 million.

Drew continues his service to our nation and maintains his Top Secret clearance as a part-time Reservist serving as a comptroller at Headquarters, Special Operations Command, Central Command. He also serves as an admissions liaison officer (ALO) for the United States Air Force Academy, where he recruits, interviews, assesses, and assists soon-to-be high school graduates from the Tampa area who aspire to attend the US Air Force Academy.

He is a graduate of the United States Air Force Academy and earned his MBA degree from Saint Leo University in St. Leo, Florida. He holds Series 7 and 66 securities licenses, plus state life and health insurance licenses.

As a First Command Financial Advisor, Drew is committed to helping his clients pursue their financial goals and lifetime dreams by bringing sound financial knowledge and trustworthy advice to a lasting relationship with each individual and family he serves. He understands the vital role a mentor/coach can serve in a person's life. He applies his experience by coaching his clients to embrace time-tested, disciplined financial strategies so they can achieve financial freedom and ensure financial security for their loved ones. He is a dedicated servant to his community, serving as a youth group leader and baseball coach.

Drew and his wife, Jessica, have one daughter, Kennedy. He is a member of the American Society of Military Comptrollers and the MacDill Air Force Base Company Grade Officer's Council. He enjoys spending time with his family and friends, reading, watching baseball and football, playing softball, jet skiing, and snowboarding.

About the Author

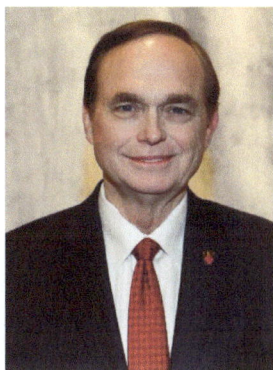

Jim Petersen, PhD, CFP®, CLF®, ChFC®, CLU®, RICP®, WMCP®, CRPC®, CAP®, CASL®, AEP®
Adjunct Professor, The American College
Bryn Mawr, Pennsylvania
jimp76@gmail.com
jlpeterseninc.com

Jim Petersen entered the financial services field in 1983 while continuing a twenty-two-year career in the United States Navy and United States Navy Reserve. He served as a submarine officer and retired with the rank of captain (0-6). As a commissioned officer in the United States Navy, he served on active duty as a nuclear submariner for seven years. His military expertise included many aspects of nuclear propulsion and submarine warfare.

Jim retired from a major financial services company at the end of 2018, having served in multiple positions in both the field and the home office. A seasoned executive with more than thirty-five years of experience in the investment and financial services industries, he is an expert in the fields of financial planning, retirement planning, and leading large financial-planning organizations.

Jim graduated from the United States Naval Academy with a bachelor of science degree, and he earned a master of science degree in management and financial services from The American College. On June 1, 2017, he became the first financial services manager to be awarded a PhD in financial and retirement planning from The American College.

He is a past president of the Alumni Board of The American College and Vice Chairman of The American College Penn Mutual Center for Veterans Affairs. He serves as an adjunct professor for The American College, specializing in comprehensive financial planning, ethics, and organizational behavior. His passion is consumer finance with an emphasis on behavioral finance.

In addition, Jim is a member of the Financial Planning Association and the Financial Services Institute. He is a member of GAMA International, an association for leadership development in the financial services industry, and is a former member of the GAMA Foundation Board of Trustees. In 2019, he was selected to receive GAMA's Cy Pick Award for his efforts as a volunteer for GAMA International.

Jim is also a life member of the United States Naval Academy Alumni Association, the Military Officers Association of America, and the Association of the United States of the United States Navy. In addition, he is a former member of the University of Tampa Board of Fellows.

Jim and his wife, Louise, have three children and two grandchildren and split their time between their homes in Fort Worth, Texas, and Orlando, Florida.

www.ingramcontent.com/pod-product-compliance
Lightning Source LLC
Chambersburg PA
CBHW041118210326
41518CB00031B/146